Micro Discipline

How to Build Unbreakable Self-Control, Crush Procrastination, and Achieve Success Through Small Daily Habits

Jordan Cross

Copyright © Jordan Cross 2025 - All rights reserved.

The content contained within this book may not be reproduced, duplicated or transmitted without direct written permission from the author or the publisher.

Under no circumstances will any blame or legal responsibility be held against the publisher, or author, for any damages, reparation, or monetary loss due to the information contained within this book. Either directly or indirectly. You are responsible for your own choices, actions, and results.

Legal Notice:

This book is copyright protected. This book is only for personal use. You cannot amend, distribute, sell, use, quote or paraphrase any part, or the content within this book, without the consent of the author or publisher.

Disclaimer Notice:

Please note the information contained within this document is for educational and entertainment purposes only. All effort has been executed to present accurate, up to date, and reliable, complete information. No warranties of any kind are declared or implied. Readers acknowledge that the author is not engaging in the rendering of legal, financial, medical or professional advice. The content within this book has been derived from various sources. Please consult a licensed professional before attempting any techniques outlined in this book.

By reading this document, the reader agrees that under no circumstances is the author responsible for any losses, direct or indirect, which are incurred as a result of the use of the information contained within this document, including, but not limited to, — errors, omissions, or inaccuracies.

Contents

Introduction: The Micro Revolution Begins	v
1. The Sabotage Code	1
2. The Micro-Mission Mindset	17
3. The Effortless Engine	31
4. Procrastination's Kryptonite	43
5. Forging the Iron Will	55
6. Invisible Habits	67
7. Chaos as Catalyst	76
8. The Scaling Secret	86
9. The Forever Framework	97
10. Mastery Unleashed	108
Conclusion: The Micro Legacy	119
Bonus: Summary & Micro Wins	127
References	133

Introduction: The Micro Revolution Begins

What if self-discipline isn't about grinding harder, but about shrinking the battlefield?

For years, we've been told that discipline is about sheer willpower—the ability to push through resistance, force ourselves to take action, and battle against procrastination. But what if the secret to self-discipline wasn't about working harder, but about removing the friction that makes action difficult in the first place?

That's exactly what one struggling freelancer discovered when her chaotic life reached a breaking point.

The 30-Second Habit That Changed Everything

Sarah was drowning.

As a freelance designer, she had no set hours, no boss breathing down her neck, and no external structure forcing her to stay productive. At first, it felt like freedom—until it didn't.

Deadlines slipped. Work piled up. Emails went unanswered. Days blurred into weeks of unproductive guilt spirals, where she promised herself to do better "tomorrow," only to find herself scrolling social media or binge-watching another Netflix show.

Sarah wasn't lazy. She cared about her work. But every time she sat down to start a project, her brain resisted. The task felt overwhelming, the stakes too high, the pressure too great. The weight of it all kept her from beginning.

One night, out of sheer frustration, she made a tiny change. Instead of forcing herself to "just start working," she committed to something absurdly small: opening a blank document and writing the project title.

That was it.

No pressure to finish anything. No expectation to complete a full section. Just a simple, effortless first step.

What happened next surprised her. The moment the document was open, the resistance faded. She figured she might as well type out the first sentence. Then another. Within ten minutes, she was deep in her work, fully engaged.

It wasn't willpower that got her moving. It was removing the mental barrier to starting. Over time, she applied the same principle elsewhere:

- Instead of committing to a full workout, she promised herself one squat.
- Instead of tackling her entire inbox, she replied to one email.
- Instead of meditating for twenty minutes, she took one deep breath.

Each small action removed resistance. And as she stacked these tiny wins, something remarkable happened—she stopped waiting for motivation and started acting out of habit.

Sarah's productivity skyrocketed, her procrastination faded, and discipline became second nature. Not through force. Not through willpower. But through a simple shift in approach. That shift is what this book is about.

My Journey to Self-Discipline

I still remember the day my younger sister, Sarah, sat me down and told me she was worried about me. She was only three years younger, but in that moment, she felt years ahead of me. She had a stable career, a life filled with purpose, and a sense of direction that I completely lacked. I was 28 years old, jobless, aimless, and drowning in an endless cycle of video games and... pornography. I kept telling myself that I will stop these bad habits *tomorrow*—but tomorrow never came.

I had convinced myself that life was just unfair, that I was somehow doomed to fail while others succeeded. I blamed the job market, the economy, and even my own bad luck. But deep down, I knew the truth: I was the problem. No one was coming to save me.

That realization hit me like a freight train one night when I looked in the mirror and barely recognized the person staring back at me. I had wasted years waiting for motivation to strike, hoping for something to change my life. But nothing changed—because I didn't change.

That was the night I decided to take control. Not with grand resolutions or overwhelming plans, but with something deceptively simple: *small, daily discipline.*

At first, it was painful. Waking up early, cutting back on screen time, forcing myself to *do the hard things* instead of lazing around. But with each tiny step forward, I felt a shift. The chains that paralyzed me—procrastination, addiction, self-doubt—began to break. I started reading about habits, psychology, and self-discipline. I committed to building something, even if I had no idea what it would turn into.

I started my first online eCommerce business, not because I had everything figured out, but because I was willing to show up *every single day* and put in the work. The success didn't come overnight, but neither did the failure that had kept me stuck for so long. Over time, discipline became second nature. I wasn't just working on a business—I was rebuilding *myself*.

Fast forward to today, I've not only built multiple six-figures online businesses, but I've also started to publish books to share what I've learned. If you had told me just a few years ago that I'd be writing a book about self-discipline, I would have laughed in your face. But now, I know firsthand that change isn't about willpower or talent—it's about consistently showing up, no matter how small the steps may seem. Showing up for YOU, YOURSELF will be the noblest decision you will ever make.

Sarah still jokes about that conversation we had years ago—the one where she sat me down and begged me to turn my life around. She tells me how proud she is, how she barely recognizes the person I used to be. And honestly? Neither do I. Because that version of me is gone.

The person writing this? He decided to *be* the change. And if you're stuck in your own cycle of self-doubt and procrastination, I hope you realize that you can be the change too. The purpose of sharing my story isn't to impress you. I'm not some multi-billionaire nor am I some top level athlete. However, I've been able to use what I share in this book to rebuild my life, look back to who I was 5 years ago and feel proud of the decisions that I've made.

Without further ado, let's first uncover the theme of this book, what discipline <u>really</u> means, and how you can maximise this book to create the change you never thought was possible for yourself.

Theme of this book

Big goals paralyze. Small steps liberate.

Your brain is wired to resist overwhelming tasks. This is why most New Year's resolutions fail within weeks—because people try to overhaul their entire lifestyle overnight.

Instead of setting massive, daunting goals, the solution is to shrink them down to their smallest possible version. Want to write a book? Start by writing one sentence. Want to get in shape? Start with one jumping jack. The easier it is to begin, the more likely you are to continue.

Redefining Discipline

Most people see discipline as a form of punishment—something unpleasant that requires suffering and sacrifice. But true discipline is the opposite. Discipline isn't restriction. It's freedom.

When you're disciplined:

- You work efficiently, which means you have more free time.
- You control your habits, instead of letting impulses control you.
- You reduce stress, because tasks don't pile up and become overwhelming.

This book is built on a simple but powerful idea: *tiny changes lead to massive results*. Instead of relying on motivation or forcing yourself to work harder, you'll learn how to reprogram your habits and environment so that self-discipline becomes automatic.

What You Will Learn:

- How to master impulse control using unconventional tools that make resisting distractions easy, or at least much easier.
- How to defeat procrastination with a simple trick that forces you to take immediate action.
- How to develop unshakable habits by leveraging the science of habit formation and micro-wins.
- How to make self-discipline automatic

Each chapter is written to build on the last, so to read it from start to end is highly recommended. Even if you read something that makes you think "Oh, I've read this before". I'd like to challenge you and ask you: "Are you living it?"

How to Use This Book

To make these principles stick, this book builds on three key pillars that will elevate your self-discipline:

• **Mindset** – Rewiring how you think about discipline and motivation.

• **Mechanics** – Implementing simple, powerful techniques to remove resistance.

• **Mastery** – Locking in these changes so they become second nature.

Each chapter ends with a section called "Quick Micro Wins". Every "Quick Micro Wins" offers 3-5 actionable ideas for you to immediately implement. Treat this book as a workbook and not one that you just read in one sitting and make no changes in real life. This isn't just a book you read. It's a book you use.

A Journey from Chaos to Control

This book is designed to be a transformation, not just information. Each chapter will help you unlock a new level of control over your time, habits, and actions. Hopefully by the end, you'll be unrecognizable—in the best way. As you turn the page, remember: *the smallest step is the mightiest leap.*

Chapter 1

The Sabotage Code

Your brain is a double agent. It is supposed to help you focus, stay disciplined, and make smart choices. Yet, time and time again, it betrays you.

You tell yourself you'll wake up early and work out, but when morning comes, you hit snooze. You block off time to write that report, yet suddenly, organizing your desk feels more urgent. You set a goal, fully intending to follow through, yet hours slip by as you scroll through your phone.

You are not alone in this struggle. The human brain, designed for survival, prioritizes comfort over challenge, short-term rewards over long-term benefits, and safety over risk. What feels like laziness or lack of discipline is often just outdated programming—one that makes productivity feel unnatural and procrastination feel inevitable.

But the brain is not an unchangeable force. The same mechanisms that make discipline difficult can be rewired to make it effortless. The key lies in understanding how your mind works, recognizing its tricks, and learning how to turn them in your favor.

The Biology of Betrayal

Your struggle with discipline is not a personal failure—it is a biological reality. The modern world has evolved far faster than the human brain, leaving us wired for a way of life that no longer exists.

Dopamine Hijack

Why does your brain choose instant gratification over progress? Every time you resist work in favor of checking your phone or watching TV, your brain is making a calculated decision—one that favors short-term pleasure over long-term success.

This decision is controlled by **dopamine**, a neurotransmitter that drives motivation and reinforces behavior. In an ancient world where survival depended on seizing every opportunity for food, shelter, and social connection, this system worked to our advantage. Today, it does not.

Modern technology hijacks this dopamine loop, bombarding fast and easy rewards at the tap of a screen. Social media, streaming services, junk food, video games. All of these modern norms triggers massive surges of dopamine without requiring any effort. The brain, wired to seek the biggest reward for the least amount of work, naturally gravitates toward these high-stimulation activities.

This is why you might find it easier to scroll endlessly through social media than to write an important email, why playing a video game feels more enticing than exercising, and why you refresh your inbox rather than start the difficult task you've been avoiding.

The result? Your brain becomes conditioned to seek instant gratification, making self-discipline feel like an uphill battle.

Rewiring this system starts with understanding one key principle: if you want to change your behavior, you must change what your brain perceives as rewarding.

The simplest way to do this is to make productivity more immediately satisfying while making distractions less accessible. Shrink your goals so that wins come faster, creating small but steady hits of dopamine that reinforce discipline. Set up barriers between yourself and distractions, removing the ease of temptation. And when possible, pair the activities you enjoy with the habits you want to build—listening to music while working out, enjoying your favorite coffee only when deep into a task—so that your brain starts to associate effort with pleasure.

Discipline is not about resisting temptation through sheer willpower. It is about designing an environment where good habits become the default choice.

Decision Fatigue

Every choice you make throughout the day depletes your mental energy. The more decisions you make, the harder it becomes to maintain self-discipline.

This is why, after a long day of work, it feels nearly impossible to cook a healthy meal or go to the gym. It is why you might start the morning focused and motivated, yet by afternoon, you find yourself procrastinating or making poor decisions.

The name for this phenomenon is decision fatigue. When the brain is overloaded with choices, it defaults to the least painful option, which is often the least productive one.

The solution is to reduce unnecessary decision-making. The fewer choices you have to make, the more mental energy you conserve for the things that truly matter.

Many of the world's highest performers—CEOs, athletes, artists—use a strategy known as pre-deciding. They eliminate small, repetitive decisions from their daily lives by setting up fixed routines. They wear the same outfit each day, eat the same breakfast, and follow the same work schedule. These seemingly minor simplifications free up enormous mental bandwidth, making it easier to focus on meaningful challenges.

You can apply this principle by automating your most frequent decisions. Set predefined rules for your daily routine. Use "if-then" strategies to eliminate hesitation—if it's morning, then you work out; if it's the weekend, then you read for thirty minutes. Remove distractions ahead of time so that the decision to focus is already made for you.

By reducing the number of choices you make each day, you leave yourself with more energy for the ones that truly count.

The Amygdala Alarm

The brain is not just wired to seek pleasure—it is also wired to avoid pain.

At the center of this avoidance system is the amygdala, the part of the brain responsible for detecting threats and triggering the stress response. In the past, this response was necessary for survival, helping us to react quickly to danger. But in today's world, it works against us.

Your amygdala cannot distinguish between a life-threatening situation and the discomfort of starting a difficult project. It only knows that a task feels overwhelming, unfamiliar, or risky, and it responds by sending stress signals that pushes you to avoid it.

This is why we hesitate before beginning a big assignment. Why we put off making an important phone call. Why we delay taking action even when you know it's in our best interests. The brain is prioritizing safety, and in doing so, it makes inaction feel more comfortable than progress.

The only way to override this response is to reframe how your brain perceives difficult tasks. Instead of focusing on the entire challenge ahead, narrow your attention to the smallest possible action. If you need to write a report, don't focus on finishing it—focus on typing the first sentence. If you need to clean your house, don't aim to finish the entire job—start by picking up one item.

By shrinking the task to something so small that it no longer triggers resistance, you bypass the amygdala's alarm system. The brain no longer perceives the action as a threat, and once you begin, momentum naturally carries you forward.

Fear fades in the face of action. The hardest part is always starting.

Your Brain Wants to Sabotage You—Unless You Take Control

The human mind is programmed to seek comfort, conserve energy, and avoid risk. It is wired for survival, not for success. Every time you delay action in favor of distraction, every time you procrastinate instead of making progress, every time you choose the easy path over the right one—it is not a lack of discipline, but a biological default.

Good news: biology is not destiny. The brain is adaptable. It can be rewired. Everytime you make the wise decision to do something that moves you towards your goals, you are rewiring it. Day by day, your brain can and will learn to do what you want it to do, with lesser and lesser resistance.

Environmental Enemies

The battle for self-discipline doesn't just take place in your mind—it plays out in your surroundings. Your environment is either an ally or an enemy in your pursuit of focus, productivity, and consistency. And more often than not, it is working against you.

When people struggle with discipline, they assume the problem is internal. They believe they need more willpower, stronger motivation, or a better mindset. But in reality, their surroundings shape their habits far more than they realize.

A cluttered space increases mental friction. Constant digital interruptions fracture focus. The people you surround yourself with either reinforce discipline or encourage distraction.

If you've ever sat down to work, only to feel overwhelmed by the mess around you, reached for your phone out of habit, or let someone else's negativity throw you off course, you've experienced how deeply the external world influences internal behavior.

Discipline is not just about personal habits—it's about environmental design. The more that your environment encourages the productive habits that drives you forward, the less effort you need to stay on track.

When Your Space Works Against You

A messy environment is more than just an aesthetic issue. Studies show that cluttered spaces increase stress, decrease focus, and make it harder to complete tasks.

When your surroundings are chaotic, your brain struggles to prioritize. Every object in your field of vision competes for attention, creating subconscious mental fatigue. The more distractions your brain has to filter out, the harder it is to focus on the work in front of you.

A study conducted at Princeton University found that physical clutter in a workspace restricts the brain's ability to focus and limits processing capacity. The more disorganized your environment, the more effort your brain must exert just to stay on task.

This explains why sitting down at a cluttered desk makes even the simplest tasks feel overwhelming. It's not just about being messy—it's about how your brain reacts to that mess.

Instead of striving for a perfectly minimalist space overnight, start with something small. Before beginning a task, clear just one inch of your workspace. Move a book, a coffee mug, or a stack of papers. Wipe down a small section of your desk. Push aside whatever is in your immediate view.

This tiny act creates a visual reset, signaling to your brain that a shift in focus is happening. Often, this small action leads to a ripple effect—once you start, you'll naturally tidy up a bit more. And with a clearer space comes a clearer mind.

During his early career, renowned chef Thomas Keller struggled with disorganization in the kitchen. His station was often cluttered, and by the end of his shift, the mess was overwhelming. It slowed him down, made tasks feel more chaotic, and left him mentally drained. His mentor, Roland Henin, introduced him to a simple but transformative rule: "Clean as you go."

Before chopping another ingredient, he wiped down his board. Before moving to a new task, he put everything back in its place. The result was immediate. Not only did his speed and efficiency improve, but he also found that he was less mentally exhausted by the end of his shift. The principle was so powerful that Keller made it a core philosophy in his own restaurants. The lesson applies beyond the kitchen. When your space is organized, your mind follows.

. . .

The Invisible Thief of Time

If clutter is the physical enemy of discipline, your phone is its digital equivalent.

The modern world is designed for interruption. Every ping, alert, and vibration demands attention, breaking focus and fracturing productivity. The average person checks their phone 150 times per day, often without even realizing it. **150 times!**

These distractions don't just consume time—they shatter deep focus. Research from the University of California, Irvine, found that when workers are interrupted, it takes an average of 23 minutes and 15 seconds to return to deep work. Multiply that across a day, and the cost is staggering.

The problem isn't just external notifications—it's the habit they create. Even when no alert goes off, many people reflexively check their phone, social media, or inbox, conditioned by years of distraction loops.

The most effective way to combat digital distractions is to create a silent bubble—a protected space where external interruptions cannot reach you. Turn off notifications completely. No banners, no sounds, no red bubbles. Set "focus hours" where you put your phone in another room. Out of sight, out of reach. Use app blockers to prevent mindless scrolling. Set restrictions for social media and entertainment apps during work hours.

The most important shift however, is internal. Each time you resist an unnecessary phone check, you reinforce control over your attention.

In 2012, venture capitalist and author Tim Ferriss realized that his productivity had taken a serious hit. He felt scattered, overwhelmed, and unable to focus deeply for long stretches. After some reflection, he traced the problem back to his smartphone. Emails, notifications, and messages were pulling his attention in dozens of directions every day.

His solution was drastic but effective. He disabled all phone notifications, checked email only twice a day, and implemented "phone-free work blocks." The results were immediate. His deep work capacity increased, his stress levels dropped, and he found that work that once took him four hours now took two.

Ferriss' experiment highlights an essential truth: our devices don't just steal time; they steal presence. The more you control the urge to check your phone, the more you regain control over your mind.

Social Saboteurs

Distraction is contagious, but so is discipline!

The people you surround yourself with influence your habits more than you think. If your friends, family, or colleagues constantly procrastinate, complain, or indulge in distractions, those behaviors become normalized.

This is known as social mirroring—the subconscious tendency to adopt the behaviors of those around us. Just as people naturally pick up accents when living in a new country, they also pick up the habits and mindset of their environment.

If you consistently spend time with people who prioritize growth, discipline, and self-improvement, their mindset will rub off on you. If you spend time with people who make excuses, indulge in negativity, or avoid hard work, those habits will also seep into your behavior.

This doesn't mean cutting everyone out of your life—it means being intentional about who you allow in your life. Imagine a smoker who is trying to quit smoking and yet 5 of his best friends that he hangs out with for hours everyday are all smokers. What's the likelihood of him *really* quitting?

Take a moment to evaluate the people you interact with most. Who in your life encourages your best habits? Who unintentionally reinforces bad habits or distractions? Who do you feel energized and inspired around? Who do you feel drained and unmotivated around?

Once you identify these patterns, make small but meaningful adjustments. Spend more time with the people who reinforce your goals. Seek out accountability partners, mentors, or communities that align with the habits you want to build. Spend less time with those who pull you toward distraction, negativity, or inconsistency. Cut these people out if possible. It's a harsh but common-sensical truth. We become who we surround ourselves with.

When motivational speaker Jim Rohn first started in business, he was surrounded by people who lacked ambition. They made excuses, avoided hard work, and dismissed the idea of self-improvement. Then he met a mentor who introduced him to a timeless principle: **"You are the average of the five people you spend the most time with."**

Taking this advice seriously, he gradually shifted his inner circle. He spent more time with successful, disciplined individuals and cut ties with those who held him back. The effect was profound. His life changed, his work ethic improved, and his business took off.

Rohn's experience is a reminder that discipline isn't just individual effort—it's shaped by the people around us.

Your Environment is Your Foundation

Self-discipline is often framed as an internal struggle, but much of it is dictated by external factors. A cluttered space creates unnecessary resistance. Digital distractions fracture attention. Social influences reinforce habits, for better or worse. None of these forces are fixed. They can all be reshaped.

When you change your environment, you change your behavior. And when discipline becomes the default choice instead of the difficult one, success follows effortlessly.

Mental Mischief

The battle for discipline isn't just fought in your environment—it happens in your mind. Even if you clear distractions, design a productive space, and surround yourself with the right people, there's still one major obstacle left: your own thoughts.

Your mind can be your greatest ally or your worst enemy. It can push you forward or hold you back. And often, it does the latter.

The way you think about discipline, success, and failure determines how consistent you are. The perfectionist who waits for the "right" time never starts. The self-critic who doubts their abilities gives up too soon. The person consumed by comparison loses motivation before they begin.

Your thoughts shape your actions. If you don't take control of them, they will sabotage your progress before you even get started.

The Perfection Paradox

If you've ever put off starting something because you weren't "ready" —because you needed more time, better skills, or the right conditions —you've fallen into the perfection trap.

Perfectionism masquerades as a noble trait. It makes you feel like you have high standards, like you won't settle for mediocrity. But in reality, perfectionism is just well-dressed procrastination. It keeps you in a cycle of overthinking, avoiding, and delaying.

The brain plays a cruel trick when it comes to perfectionism. It tells you that you need more preparation before you start. But the truth is, **you don't become ready by waiting—you become ready by doing.**

Consider Leonardo da Vinci, one of history's greatest artists and inventors. He had a habit of delaying projects, obsessing over perfecting every detail. His most famous work, the *Mona Lisa*, took him four years to paint—and even then, he never considered it truly finished. Some of his other projects never saw completion at all. While his genius was undeniable, his perfectionism often slowed his progress.

Contrast this with Pablo Picasso, who produced more than 50,000 works of art in his lifetime. He understood that creating imperfect work was the key to growth. Instead of getting stuck on one project, he focused on volume, trusting that mastery would emerge through repetition.

The lesson? **Done beats perfect.** While both are geniuses in their own ways, most of us are never going to have the innate talent that Leonardo has. Our best bet would be to be as relentless as Picasso. The best way to improve is to start before you feel ready.

The Messy Start Trick

If you struggle with perfectionism, the solution is simple: lower the bar.

Start by giving yourself permission to create something *bad*. Write a terrible first draft. Make a rough, unfinished sketch. Begin the workout with just five minutes of movement. The goal is momentum, not mastery.

Once you begin, your brain's resistance lowers. Perfectionism loses its grip. And before you know it, you've taken the first step toward progress.

Self-Talk Traps

The way you speak to yourself determines how disciplined you become.

Studies show that 80% of thoughts are self-critical. Crazy, right? Your inner voice constantly judges, doubts, and second-guesses. It tells you that you're not disciplined enough, not smart enough, not capable enough. Over time, this self-talk creates a mental barrier that keeps you from even trying.

Athletes, performers, and high achievers understand the power of self-talk. Muhammad Ali didn't just train his body—he trained his mind. He constantly repeated, "I am the greatest," long before he had the titles to prove it. His words shaped his reality.

In contrast, those who tell themselves, "I'm bad at this," or "I never follow through," reinforce those identities. The brain listens to what we repeatedly say and adjusts our behavior accordingly.

If you want to build discipline, you have to level up your internal dialogue.

Flipping Negative Self-Talk

Instead of saying:

- "I'm not disciplined." → Say: "I am learning to be disciplined every day."
- "I always procrastinate." → Say: "I am working toward taking action sooner."

- "I never finish what I start." → Say: "I follow through more than I used to."

The key is subtle shifts. Your brain won't believe a radical lie, but it will accept a small, progressive improvement. Your words do become your identity. Choose them carefully.

Back when I was down deep in my addictions, I had to completely uproot my negative and disempowering self-talks. One mantra that I repeated dozens if not hundreds of times everyday for hundreds of days straight is "I do it NOW". "I do it NOW" nudged me to do more, push more, resist a little longer, persist a little longer. "I do it NOW" worked so well for me because of how often I delay things. Find your own mantra!

The Comparison Con

Nothing kills discipline faster than comparing your progress to someone else's.

Social media has made this worse. You see people achieving big milestones—buying houses, getting promotions, traveling the world—while you feel stuck in place. The brain interprets this as evidence that you're falling behind.

But comparison is an illusion. What you see is only the highlight reel, not the struggle behind the scenes. You don't see the late nights, the failures, the doubts, and the sacrifices that led to those moments of success.

The musician Ed Sheeran once shared that when he started writing songs, he was *terrible*. His early lyrics were embarrassing, his melodies were clumsy. But he kept writing, producing hundreds of songs until he got better. If he had compared himself to more established artists early on, he might have given up. Instead, he focused on his own progress.

How to Stay Focused on Your Own Path

If you catch yourself comparing, shift your focus inward. Instead of measuring yourself against someone else's journey, measure yourself against your **past self**.

- Are you more disciplined today than you were last year?
- Are you showing up for yourself more consistently?
- Are you making small improvements, even if they're not visible yet?

The only path that matters is your own. Stay focused on it.

Quick Micro Wins

Discipline isn't built overnight, but small victories compound into lasting change. To apply everything you've learned in this chapter, start with these five actions:

1. **Eliminate a single environmental distraction.** Remove one thing from your workspace that contributes to clutter or mental fatigue—clear your desk, turn off notifications, or move your phone to another room while working.
2. **Break a big goal into a micro-action.** If you've been delaying something, reduce it to a task so small that it feels effortless to start. Instead of "write a chapter," commit to writing one sentence. Instead of "start working out," commit to one push-up.

3. **Reframe one self-defeating thought.** Catch yourself in a negative mental loop and replace it with a phrase that reinforces progress. Change "I'll do it tomorrow" to "I do it NOW."
4. **Take a 24-hour digital detox.** If your phone or social media is hijacking your focus, remove the temptation for one full day. Notice how it impacts your mental clarity and attention span.
5. **Audit your circle.** Identify the people in your life who influence your discipline. Who pushes you forward? Who pulls you back? Make an intentional effort to spend more time with those who reinforce your best habits.

Each of these actions takes minutes, but their impact lasts far longer.

Discipline isn't about working harder—it's about removing friction, reprogramming your mindset, and setting yourself up for success before you even begin. Now that you understand the forces sabotaging your progress, it's time to take back control.

Chapter 2

The Micro-Mission Mindset

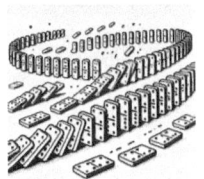

A single push-up changed Stephen Guise's life.

It wasn't part of an intense workout plan. There was no pressure, no expectation of transformation. He simply told himself he would do one push-up. That was it. The next day, he did another. Then another. Soon, one push-up became five. Then ten. Then twenty. A year later, he had a fitness routine that felt as natural as brushing his teeth.

What made this approach so powerful? He never focused on the long-term goal. He never told himself he had to "get in shape" or "build muscle." He only committed to one small action each day.

Most people approach discipline the wrong way. They set big, overwhelming goals—lose 50 pounds, write a novel, wake up at 5 AM every day—and then struggle when motivation fades. They believe self-discipline is about forcing themselves through resistance. But the truth is, the brain resists anything that feels too large, too difficult, or too uncertain.

The key to lasting discipline isn't willpower. It's momentum. And momentum starts small.

The Micro-Mission Mindset is about shrinking your goals until they're too small to fail. Instead of focusing on big results, you focus on tiny, consistent actions. Instead of waiting for motivation, you create a system that keeps you moving forward, no matter how small the steps.

Tiny changes lead to massive transformations.

The Power of Tiny

The biggest enemy of discipline is **resistance**. When a task feels too big, the brain triggers stress, leading to procrastination. The trick to slip past it? Micro tasks.

In behavioral science, this is called the **"low friction" principle**—the idea that if something feels effortless, you're more likely to do it. Once you take action, even the tiniest step, momentum takes over.

When author James Clear studied habit formation, he found that a habit needs to be as easy as possible at first—under two minutes—to become sustainable. He called this the Two-Minute Rule: if you want to build a habit, make the first step ridiculously easy. Want to start reading more? Read one sentence. Want to meditate daily? Sit down for ten seconds. Want to run a marathon? Put on your running shoes.

The easier the action, the easier it is to start. And once you start, the brain naturally wants to continue.

British cycling coach Dave Brailsford used this principle to transform the British cycling team. Instead of overhauling everything at once, he looked for small, **1% improvements**, adjusting seat positioning, optimizing nutrition, and improving sleep quality. Each improvement was minor, but together, they compounded into a massive performance boost. Within five years, British cyclists dominated the Olympics.

Small wins, repeated consistently, create exponential results.

If you're struggling with discipline, don't think about the end goal. Think about the next smallest action you can take. Write one sentence. Do one push-up. Save one dollar. A single step is all you need to start building momentum.

The Compound Effect

A 1% improvement doesn't seem like much. It's barely noticeable. But over time, small improvements stack up into life-changing results.

Imagine improving by just 1% every day. At first, it won't seem like much. But thanks to the power of compounding, after one year, you won't be just a little better. You'll be 37 times better than where you started.

The problem is that most people want instant results. They expect massive progress within days, and when they don't see it, they quit. But real success follows an exponential curve—slow, slow, slow... then suddenly huge.

Most people give up just before their breakthrough. They plant the seed but don't stick around long enough to see it grow.

Warren Buffett, one of the world's richest men, didn't become a billionaire overnight. He started investing at age 11. For decades, his net worth grew slowly. By age 52, he was worth $376 million—awesome, but far from legendary.

Then compounding kicked in. At 60, he was worth $3.8 billion. At 70, $36 billion. Today, he's worth over $100 billion. The majority of his fortune came after his 60s—not because he made drastic changes, but because he allowed the magic of compounding to happen over time.

Consistency beats intensity. A 1% improvement today doesn't look like much, but over time, it changes everything.

Why Big Goals Make You Quit

The brain resists big, vague goals. "Get in shape," "become more productive," or "start a business" sound great in theory, but they overwhelm the brain in practice.

Neuroscientist Dr. BJ Fogg discovered that people are more likely to stick to a habit when they start small—so small that resistance disappears. He called this "Tiny Habits."

When one of his students wanted to start flossing daily, Fogg told him to floss just one tooth. That's it. No pressure to do more. Within weeks, the habit expanded naturally.

The same strategy works for any goal. If something feels overwhelming, shrink it down until it feels effortless.

A university student struggling with assignments always felt too overwhelmed to start. Deadlines loomed, but the tasks felt too big. Then he changed his approach. Instead of thinking, *I need to finish this entire essay,* he set a micro-mission: *I will write one sentence.*

The resistance vanished. Writing one sentence was easy. Once he wrote the first sentence, the next one came naturally. Before he knew it, he was deep into the assignment.

This method, called the **one-bite rule**, works for anything.

- Don't clean your whole house—just wash one dish.
- Don't read a whole book—just read one paragraph.
- Don't run a mile—just jog for ten seconds.

By shrinking the task, you remove the mental roadblocks stopping you from taking action.

Small Steps, Big Leaps

Discipline isn't about forcing yourself to work harder. It's about making action feel effortless.

The secret to consistency isn't motivation. It's reducing resistance so that taking action feels easy.

If you've struggled with discipline in the past, it's not because you're weak or lazy. It's because the goal was too big. The trick is to start so small that failure becomes impossible.

One sentence. One push-up. One action at a time.

Success isn't built in a day, but it is built daily. And it always starts with something small.

Redefining Ambition

Most people believe success requires massive effort, extreme discipline, and relentless willpower. They set ambitious goals—run a marathon, write a book, build a thriving business—and then struggle under the weight of their own expectations.

The problem isn't their ambition. It's the scale of their starting point.

Big goals create big resistance. They trigger anxiety, hesitation, and overthinking. The brain sees a mountain and freezes, unsure where to start.

But what if ambition isn't about setting bigger goals? What if it's about setting *smaller* ones—so small that success becomes inevitable?

This is the paradox of high achievement: the people who accomplish the most don't start with massive leaps. They start with tiny steps that compound over time.

The Shrink Strategy

Tim Ferriss, bestselling author of *The 4-Hour Workweek*, once shared his secret for writing books: he never sets out to write a book. Instead, he writes *two pages per day*.

That's it. No pressure to craft a masterpiece. No overwhelming goal of writing 300 pages. Just two imperfect pages, every single day.

By shrinking the goal, he removes resistance. Two pages feel easy, almost too easy. But those pages add up. After 150 days, he has a 300-page manuscript.

This approach works for anything.

Brandon Sanderson, a prolific fantasy author, follows a similar method. Instead of pressuring himself to write full chapters, he sets a daily target of just 50 words—not 500, not 1,000. Just 50.

Most days, he writes far more. But even on the hardest days, he hits his target. Within a year, his book is finished.

When you cut your goals down to 1/10th their size, two things happen:

1. The task feels too small to resist.
2. Consistency becomes automatic.

Small, consistent progress is far more powerful than bursts of motivation. If a goal feels intimidating, shrink it. Instead of:

- "I need to write a book" → Write 50 words a day
- "I need to exercise daily" → Do one push-up
- "I need to start a side business" → Work for five minutes

Less is more in self-discipline. And small always beats stalled.

The Success Snowball

Success is addictive.

Each time you complete a task—even a small one—your brain releases dopamine, the neurochemical of motivation. This creates a powerful feedback loop: **progress feels good, so you want to keep going.**

This is why people get hooked on video games. Games are designed to deliver constant small wins—leveling up, unlocking rewards, progressing toward the next milestone. The brain craves these victories.

You can use this psychology to your advantage by creating a *win log*—a simple way to track every small success.

Jordan Syatt, a fitness coach and former powerlifting champion, once trained a client named Emily, who had spent years struggling with weight loss. Every diet she tried felt overwhelming. Every workout plan felt unsustainable.

So they changed their approach.

Instead of obsessing over losing 100 pounds, Emily tracked small wins: drinking one extra glass of water, walking for five minutes, eating one healthy meal. Each tiny win built confidence. Each success reinforced her identity as a disciplined person. Over time, her momentum snowballed. And eventually, the weight came off—not because she forced herself to be "perfect," but because she built a system where wins were inevitable.

The same strategy applies to any goal.

Before Ed Sheeran became one of the best-selling musicians in the world, he was an unknown teenager in the UK, trying to improve his songwriting. At first, his lyrics were rough, his melodies were unpolished. Instead of waiting to feel "ready," he focused on one goal: write one song per day.

Most of them were terrible. But he kept going. Over time, his songwriting improved. His confidence grew. He played small gigs, then bigger ones. He recorded music, built an audience, and eventually, his career took off.

He didn't wait for motivation. He didn't set out to write a hit song overnight. He simply tracked his small wins and let them build momentum.

If you want discipline to feel effortless, track your wins. Each small victory reinforces the belief that you are making progress—and nothing fuels consistency like visible success.

The Anti-Overwhelm Shield

One of the biggest mistakes people make when pursuing self-discipline is trying to do too much at once.

Multitasking, overloaded to-do lists, and unrealistic expectations create stress, not progress.

The science is clear: multitasking reduces efficiency, increases errors, and burns out the brain. Researchers at Stanford University found that people who multitask are **40% less productive** than those who focus on one task at a time.

Instead of trying to tackle everything at once, high performers focus on *single-tasking*. They don't try to do ten things at once. They zoom in on one clear, specific task and give it their full attention.

Most people try to juggle everything, and as a result, they achieve nothing. The secret to sustainable success is relentless focus.

If you want to avoid burnout, adopt the *micro-mission mindset*:

- Instead of "I need to be more productive," focus on completing one important task today.
- Instead of "I need to get in shape," focus on doing one workout this week.
- Instead of "I need to change my life," focus on changing one small habit at a time.

One clear, focused mission at a time. That's the key to long-term success.

Small is Sustainable, and Sustainable is Unstoppable

Most people overestimate what they can do in a day and underestimate what they can do in a year. They set goals that are too big, try to do too much at once, and burn out before they make real progress.

The Micro-Mission Mindset flips this equation.

By shrinking your goals, tracking tiny wins, and focusing on one small mission at a time, you remove resistance, build momentum, and make success inevitable.

You don't need more discipline. You need a system that makes discipline easy. Start small. Stay consistent. Let the results take care of themselves.

Making It Stick

Starting is one thing. Sticking with it is another.

Most people don't struggle with taking action once—they struggle with taking action *consistently*. They build momentum for a few days, maybe even a few weeks, but then life gets in the way. A busy day throws them off track. Motivation fades. Before they know it, they're back to square one, wondering why their discipline never lasts.

This isn't a personal failing. It's a system failure.

For most, habits don't stick because they require too much painful effort. And anything that requires painful effort eventually meets resistance. But when habits become painlessly effortless—when they become automatic—they last.

The secret to lasting discipline isn't trying harder. It's **removing friction** so that good habits happen naturally, without willpower.

Habit Anchors

One of the easiest ways to make habits stick is to *tie them to something you already do*.

Every day, you brush your teeth, drink coffee, check your phone, put on your shoes. These actions happen on autopilot because they are anchored to existing routines. By attaching new habits to these built-in behaviors, you piggyback on an established rhythm—turning a new habit into an effortless extension of your day.

This strategy, called **habit stacking**, was coined by productivity expert BJ Fogg. He found that people are more likely to stick to habits when they attach them to something familiar.

- Instead of saying, *"I'll stretch every day,"* say, *"After I brush my teeth, I'll do a 30-second stretch."*
- Instead of saying, *"I'll start journaling,"* say, *"After I pour my morning coffee, I'll write one sentence."*

A mother of three who struggled to find time for self-care used this strategy to start meditating daily. Instead of trying to carve out a separate time for meditation, she linked it to something automatic: *waiting for the microwave.* Every time she microwaved food—whether it was heating up her coffee or making lunch for her kids—she used that time to close her eyes and breathe.

At first, it was just 30 seconds. But it became a ritual. A few deep breaths turned into a mindful moment. That mindful moment turned into two minutes. Soon, meditation became part of her routine, without any extra effort.

The easiest way to make habits stick is to **tie them to something you already do.** When the trigger is automatic, the habit follows effortlessly.

The 2-Minute Rule

Most habits fail because they feel *too much.*

Going to the gym feels too much. Writing a chapter feels too much. Meditating for 20 minutes feels too much.

The brain resists anything that feels *"too much"*. But it has no problem doing something that takes *only two minutes.*

David Allen, author of *Getting Things Done*, discovered that if a task takes less than two minutes, it's *too small to procrastinate.* The key is starting with an action so tiny that resistance disappears.

- If you want to exercise, just put on your workout clothes.
- If you want to read more, read one sentence.
- If you want to clean your room, fold one shirt.

A software engineer who struggled to build a daily coding habit used this method to break through resistance. Instead of committing to hours of deep work, he told himself, *"I'll just write one line of code."*

That's it.

Once he wrote one line, it was easier to keep going. Most days, that single line turned into 10 minutes, then 30, then an hour. But even on bad days, he wrote *something*.

This is the power of the 2-Minute Rule. The hardest part of any task is starting. Once you're in motion, momentum takes over.

Why Rewards Make Habits Stick

Most people focus on *building* habits but forget about *reinforcing* them.

The brain thrives on rewards. Every time you accomplish something, your brain releases dopamine—the neurochemical of motivation. Without this reward, habits fade. But when habits feel rewarding, they stick.

Celebration is how you tell your brain, *This action is worth repeating*.

The problem is, most people only reward big accomplishments. They wait until they've lost 10 pounds before they celebrate. They wait until they've finished a book before they feel proud.

But the brain doesn't respond to delayed rewards. It responds to **immediate** wins.

A teacher who wanted to become more consistent with her lesson planning struggled to stay disciplined. She always felt drained by the end of the day. So she started using a simple trick: after every 30-minute planning session, she played her favorite song as a reward.

It was small, but it worked. Her brain began associating the task with something enjoyable. Planning no longer felt like a chore—it felt like a win.

If you want habits to last, build a celebration circuit:

- After completing a habit, do something enjoyable.
- Say something encouraging to yourself. ("Nice job!" works wonders.)
- Keep track of streaks. Seeing progress builds motivation.

A habit reinforced with a reward is a habit that sticks.

Quick Micro Wins

If you want to solidify the lessons from this chapter, here are three quick actions you can take right now:

1. **Anchor a new habit to an existing routine.** Think of something you already do daily—brushing your teeth, drinking coffee, putting on your shoes—and attach a micro habit to it.
2. **Use the 2-Minute Rule to break through resistance.** Whatever habit you've been avoiding, shrink it down to something that takes two minutes or less. Write one sentence, do one push-up, floss one tooth.
3. **Create an instant reward system.** Choose a simple, enjoyable way to celebrate small wins—play a song after a

task, mark an "X" on a calendar, or say "Nice work!" to yourself.

Small, consistent actions can turn into lifelong habits. Discipline isn't about forcing yourself to work harder. It's about designing your life so that good habits happen naturally.

Chapter 3

The Effortless Engine

Most people start new habits with enthusiasm. They commit to waking up early, going to the gym, writing every day, or eating healthier. But within weeks—or even days—the habit fades. Motivation wears off, obstacles appear, and life gets in the way.

Studies show that over 85% of people abandon their habits within a month. The problem isn't effort—it's reliance on effort.

If you need immense willpower to sustain a habit everyday, it won't last long.

The secret to lifelong discipline isn't pushing harder. It's making discipline the default. The most consistent people in the world—elite athletes, successful entrepreneurs, high performers—don't rely solely on motivation. They design systems that make success automatic.

You don't wake up every morning and debate whether or not to brush your teeth. You just do it. It's part of your routine, not a choice. Imagine if all your good habits worked the same way.

This chapter will show you how to build an effortless engine, so your best habits happen naturally, without thinking.

The Automation Advantage

Willpower is unreliable. Some days, you feel energized and driven. Other days, you're exhausted and tempted to quit. If your discipline depends on how you feel, consistency will always be a struggle.

Captain Chesley "Sully" Sullenberger, the pilot behind the miraculous Hudson River landing, didn't rely on willpower when his plane lost both engines. He relied on systems.

For decades, Sully had drilled emergency procedures. He didn't have to think about what to do—his training took over. In just over three minutes, he and his co-pilot executed a flawless emergency landing, saving 155 lives.

When habits are systemized, they happen automatically, no motivation required.

One of the easiest ways to build automatic habits is to design a structured morning sequence. Instead of deciding when to work out, exercise at the same time every day. Instead of debating when to journal, write immediately after making coffee. Instead of wondering what to do first at work, start with a fixed routine.

An airline pilot used this strategy to maintain discipline despite his unpredictable travel schedule. Every morning, no matter what country he was in, he followed the same five-minute morning sequence:

1. Drink a glass of water.
2. Do 10 push-ups.
3. Review his daily goals.

4. Read one page of a book.
5. Start his work for the day.

It was simple. And because it was automatic, it kept him consistent, even in chaotic environments and shifting time zones. When habits are part of a routine, they stop feeling like work. They just happen.

The Consistency Code

Self-discipline isn't about strength—it's about training.

Just like muscles grow through repeated workouts, habits become automatic through repetition.

Research shows that it takes an average of 66 days to fully automate a habit. The key is to maintain consistency long enough for your brain to rewire itself. Now note: intensity and frequency of course matters. But to simplify, take 66 days as a great benchmark for a new discipline formation.

When artist Stephen Wiltshire was a child, he was nearly nonverbal due to autism. But he had an extraordinary talent—he could draw anything he saw, down to the finest detail. He honed this ability through daily repetition.

Each day, he drew cityscapes, refining his technique. His discipline wasn't forced—it became second nature. Eventually, he became known as "The Human Camera," able to sketch entire cities from memory after a single viewing. His talent wasn't just natural—it was trained through relentless consistency.

Even though most of us do not have the talents of Stephen, we can still apply the same principle that brought him results. Showing up everyday, no matter what.

Another important pillar to consistency is tracking progress.

A comedian once asked Jerry Seinfeld for advice on becoming a better writer. Seinfeld's response?

"Write a joke every day, and don't break the chain."

He suggested marking an "X" on a calendar every day he wrote a joke. The longer the streak, the harder it became to skip a day. This strategy works because the brain hates breaking patterns. Once you build a streak, you feel compelled to maintain it.

If you want a habit to stick, track it visually.

- Use a habit-tracking app to record daily wins.
- Mark an "X" on a physical calendar every day you complete your habit.
- Create a challenge for yourself, such as "30 days of running" or "100 days of writing."

Repetition rewires the brain. If you can maintain a streak for 66 days, your habit becomes second nature.

The Power of an Effortless System

Most people give up on their disciplines because they try to force it instead of designing a system that makes discipline easy.

When disciplines are built into routines, when decisions are minimized, and when behaviors are repeated long enough to become automatic, self-control is no longer a struggle—it's a lifestyle. Use your creativity to make the right decision, the easy decision.

The goal isn't to rely on willpower. The goal is to create an environment where disciplined actions take place naturally. Design the system, and the results will take care of themselves.

Friction Fighters

A big part of creating an environment that breeds discipline is removing resistance. The easier an action feels, the more likely you are to do it.

Many people assume they struggle with consistency because they lack motivation, but more often than not, they are battling friction—the small obstacles that make good habits harder to stick to.

If your workout clothes are buried under a pile of laundry, exercising becomes an extra chore before it even begins. If your phone sits next to your bed, scrolling through social media is easily going to be the first thing you do in the morning, even if you intend to start the day with a healthier habit. If your workspace is cluttered, distractions multiply, making focus feel like an uphill battle.

Success is often less about pushing through resistance and more about clearing the path ahead. When the right choices are the easiest ones to make, discipline happens naturally.

Making Action Easy

Every habit has a starting cost. If getting started requires too much effort, procrastination follows. The key is lowering that cost so the first step feels effortless.

When science fiction writer Andy Weir was writing *The Martian*, he didn't set out to write a novel. He didn't even plan to publish a book. Instead, he started a small blog where he posted short chapters for a small group of readers. There was no pressure to create a masterpiece —just an easy habit of writing and sharing small pieces consistently.

By keeping the process friction-free, he built momentum. Eventually, those chapters became a full novel. The book went on to become a bestseller and was later adapted into a Hollywood film.

The same principle applies to any habit. The smaller and easier the first step, the more likely you are to follow through. If you want to work out, lay out your gym clothes the night before. If you want to drink more water, keep a glass on your desk. If you want to eat healthier, have pre-cut fruits and vegetables ready to grab from the fridge.

Momentum begins with small, low-effort actions. By removing obstacles, you take the hardest part—getting started—out of the equation.

Shaping Your Environment for Discipline

When things are in order, productivity flows naturally. When they aren't, even simple tasks feel overwhelming.

During his university years, psychology student Daniel Simons struggled with focus. His apartment was noisy, his desk was cluttered, and distractions were always within reach. Frustrated with his lack of progress, he made one change—he created a dedicated space for deep work. He cleared his desk, removed everything unrelated to his studies, and moved his workspace away from his bed and television.

Within days, he noticed a shift. His mind associated that space with focus, and distractions no longer pulled him away as easily. Studying became more automatic.

If you want to improve your habits, your environment should support them. Keep your workspace clean, designate specific areas for different tasks, and make distractions harder to reach. The less friction between you and the right action, the easier discipline becomes.

. . .

Reclaiming Control Over Technology

Technology is one of the biggest sources of friction for discipline. It hijacks attention, drains time, and keeps people in endless distraction loops. Most people don't struggle with being disciplined because they lack motivation—they struggle because their phone is designed to keep them hooked.

A business consultant named Lisa spent years trying to focus better at work, but she always found herself losing time to notifications, emails, and social media. Instead of trying to rely on self-control, she redesigned her approach. She deleted all non-essential apps from her phone, set "no-phone" work hours in the morning, and placed her device in another room while she worked.

The result? Within a few weeks, she regained hours of focus. The urge to check her phone weakened, and deep work became easier.

For anyone struggling with digital distractions, making a few simple changes can create an immediate impact. Turning off notifications, using website blockers, or setting phone-free hours can create an environment where focus comes naturally instead of feeling like a battle.

Removing Friction to Make Discipline Effortless

People often believe they need more motivation to be disciplined, but in reality, they need less resistance. By eliminating unnecessary obstacles, making good habits easier to start, and controlling distractions before they take over, discipline becomes a natural part of life rather than something that needs to be constantly forced.

When friction is removed, consistency follows. And when consistency becomes effortless, discipline no longer feels like work.

The Flow Trigger

Peak performers—athletes, musicians, writers, and entrepreneurs—describe moments when time seems to slow down, distractions fade, and their work feels effortless. This mental state is called *flow*.

In flow, the brain operates at its highest level. Psychologist Mihaly Csikszentmihalyi, who coined the term, found that when people are in a state of flow, their productivity triples, their creativity skyrockets, and their sense of effort disappears.

But flow doesn't just happen by accident. It can be triggered deliberately.

The good news? You don't need to be a world-class performer to experience it. Flow can be designed into your daily routine with the right habits.

The Power of a Pre-Work Trigger

Flow doesn't happen on demand. It needs a **cue**—a small, consistent action that signals to your brain that it's time to focus.

World-renowned pianist Glenn Gould had an unusual ritual before performing—he soaked his arms in hot water. This wasn't about warming up his muscles. It was a mental cue, a signal to his brain that it was time to enter a deep state of focus.

Austrian composer Franz Joseph Haydn had his own ritual. Before composing, he placed his favorite ring on his finger, then sat down at the piano. The act of wearing the ring signaled to his mind that it was time to create. This small, seemingly trivial action trained his brain to enter work mode automatically.

This method isn't just for musicians. Anyone can use a ritual to cue their brain into deep focus.

One writer, struggling with consistency, developed a ritual to trigger his writing sessions. Every morning, he made a cup of coffee, took three deep breaths, and sat at his desk. At first, it felt like a forced routine, but within weeks, his brain began to recognize this as a transition into work. Writing became easier—not because he was more disciplined, but because his brain learned to associate the act of making coffee and breathing deeply with entering a focused state.

The right pre-work ritual can transform your ability to focus.

It could be as simple as:

- Drinking tea before writing.
- Taking five deep breaths before opening your laptop.
- Playing the same instrumental song before studying.

What matters is consistency. The brain learns through repetition. If you follow the same steps every time you start deep work, your brain will begin associating those cues with focus.

Flow begins with a signal. Find yours.

Why Narrowing Attention Unlocks Effortless Work

Distraction is flow's greatest enemy. In a world of notifications, emails, and constant interruptions, the ability to *focus on one thing* is a rare and powerful skill.

Neuroscientists have found that multitasking is a myth. The brain doesn't truly do two things at once—it rapidly switches between tasks, creating mental fatigue and reducing efficiency.

Dr. Atul Gawande, a renowned surgeon and writer, follows a strict focus system before every operation. He and his team use a structured checklist to eliminate unnecessary thoughts and distractions. By the time he begins surgery, his attention is locked in. His world shrinks to a single point of focus.

The same principle applies to any deep work. To enter flow, you must eliminate competing inputs and direct all attention to one task.

A simple way to do this is by using the **One-Thing Rule**:

1. Identify the single most important task you need to complete.
2. Remove everything else from view—close extra browser tabs, silence notifications, clear your workspace.
3. Set a timer and commit to working on that one thing for a fixed time.

The first few minutes may feel slow, but as distractions fade, your mind locks in. Within 15-20 minutes, you'll feel your focus deepening.

The narrower your attention, the deeper your flow.

How to End Work Without Losing Momentum

Many people sabotage their productivity without realizing it—not by how they *start* work, but by how they *end* it.

If you stop working abruptly, your brain holds onto unfinished tasks, keeping your mind restless. But if you exit work intentionally, you close the mental loop, preserving energy and making it easier to restart the next day.

Bill Gates, known for his deep focus, follows a **shutdown ritual** at the end of each workday. Before leaving his office, he reviews what he accomplished, writes down his top priorities for the next day, and mentally closes out unfinished tasks. This simple practice allows him to unplug completely, preventing burnout and ensuring he returns the next day with clarity.

A software developer named Thomas, who struggled with focus, found that implementing an end-of-work ritual transformed his productivity. Instead of stopping work randomly, he now follows a short **shutdown script**:

1. Review what he completed.
2. List the top task for the next session.
3. Tidy his workspace to remove distractions.

By ending with intention, he eliminated mental clutter, making it easier to dive into deep work the next day.

The way you exit determines how strong your next session begins.

Quick Micro Wins

If you want to make discipline easier and more automatic, here are five immediate actions you can take:

1. **Design a simple morning routine.** Start your day with a structured sequence of habits—such as drinking water, stretching, or reviewing your goals—so discipline begins before distractions take over.
2. **Reduce decision fatigue.** Automate small choices in your daily life—like planning meals in advance, setting a fixed start time for work, or wearing the same outfit—so you have more energy for important decisions.
3. **Create a focus ritual.** Choose a small action—such as making coffee, stretching, or lighting a candle—that signals to your brain that it's time to enter deep work mode. Consistency is key.

4. **Implement a shutdown ritual.** End each work session by reviewing what you accomplished and setting up the next day's top priority. This helps clear your mind, reduces stress, and makes it easier to start strong tomorrow.

Discipline doesn't need to be forced. When you remove friction, automate decisions, and design routines that make focus feel effortless, consistency follows naturally.

Chapter 4
Procrastination's Kryptonite

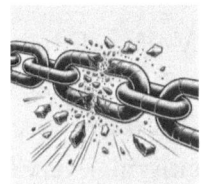

Deadlines often feel like chains—stressful, restrictive, and overwhelming. Many people see them as something to avoid, stretch, or fear. But what if deadlines weren't the enemy? What if they were actually the secret to unlocking action?

The truth is, procrastination thrives in open-ended time. When there's no urgency, the brain relaxes. It pushes things off, convincing itself that there's always *tomorrow*. But when a deadline is near, suddenly, things get done.

A research study from MIT found that students who were given evenly spaced deadlines throughout a semester performed significantly better than those given one large deadline at the end. The reason? Time pressure forces action.

Deadlines, when used strategically, can become a superpower. They can turn hesitation into momentum and transform overwhelming tasks into structured progress. This chapter will show you how to harness them, so instead of running from pressure, you use it to your advantage.

Reverse Deadlines

Most people approach deadlines the wrong way—they see a big task, estimate how long it will take, and work toward the deadline *forward*. But this method often leads to underestimating effort, last-minute panic, and rushed results.

A better strategy? Work *backward*.

Professional event planner Melissa Torres had a reputation for never missing a deadline, no matter how chaotic the project. Her secret was simple: she never started with *today*. Instead, she worked from the final moment backward, identifying every key step along the way.

If an event was scheduled for October 15, she asked:

- What absolutely must be finished by October 14?
- What needs to be done a week before that?
- What should be completed a month prior?

By mapping out checkpoints *in reverse*, she eliminated the uncertainty of where to start. She broke massive tasks into smaller, time-sensitive pieces.

Reverse deadlines work because they force clarity. Instead of guessing how long a task will take, you pinpoint exactly when each piece must be done to hit the final goal with ease.

The next time you're faced with a daunting project, try this method:

1. Set the final deadline—when the task must be completed.
2. Work backward to identify milestone deadlines.
3. Assign specific actions to each checkpoint.

This approach removes guesswork and prevents the last-minute scramble.

Deadlines stop feeling like pressure—they start working *for* you.

Why Work Expands to Fill the Time You Give It

Parkinson's Law states that work expands to fill the time available for its completion. If you give yourself a week to complete a task, it will take a week. If you give yourself a day, suddenly, you'll find a way to make it happen in a day.

This is why students who have months to write a paper often complete 80% of the work the night before it's due—and why employees who have an entire afternoon to finish a simple report somehow take the entire afternoon.

A college senior named Ben experienced this firsthand. Every semester, he told himself he'd start studying early for finals, yet every semester, he found himself cramming the night before the exam.

Frustrated with his cycle of procrastination, he decided to *manufacture* urgency. Instead of waiting until the last minute, he artificially shortened his study window. He set deadlines two weeks before his actual exams, treating them as if they were the real test dates.

The result? He worked with greater focus, avoided stress, and performed better than ever before.

By shrinking the time available for a task, you force yourself to work efficiently.

If you often find yourself stretching tasks longer than necessary, set **artificial constraints**:

- If you normally take three hours to complete a report, try doing it in 90 minutes.

- If a presentation deadline is in two weeks, set a personal due date for this Friday.

Tighter clocks crush procrastination.

Beating Procrastination with a Timer

One of the hardest parts of overcoming procrastination is simply starting. The longer you hesitate, the harder it gets.

A novelist named Laura Monroe struggled with writer's block for years. She had stories in her head but could never get past the first page. Every time she sat down to write, doubt crept in. She overthought every sentence, deleted paragraphs, and ended up with nothing.

Her breakthrough came when she discovered the five-minute countdown trick. Instead of pressuring herself to write an entire chapter, she told herself she only had to write for five minutes—no matter how bad it was.

She set a countdown timer, put her hands on the keyboard, and started. At first, she barely wrote anything. But by the time the five minutes were up, something had changed—she was in motion. The fear of starting was gone.

She didn't stop at five minutes. She kept going.

This trick works because it bypasses the brain's resistance to starting. Five minutes is *too small* to feel intimidating. Once movement begins, momentum takes over.

If you struggle with procrastination, try this:

1. Set a five-minute countdown timer.
2. Work on the task until the timer runs out.

3. When the time is up, decide if you want to stop or keep going.

Most of the time, you'll keep going. The hardest part isn't the work—it's getting started.

The Action Antidote

Procrastination thrives in stillness. The longer you wait, the harder it becomes to start. The brain builds up tasks in the mind, making them seem bigger than they are. It hesitates, looks for distractions, and convinces itself that the perfect time to begin is *later*. But later never comes.

The solution? Start before you feel ready.

Action precedes motivation—not the other way around. The moment you move, resistance weakens. The brain shifts from thinking to doing. Momentum builds.

This section will show you how to trick your mind into action, bypass perfectionism, and use physics to your advantage.

The Power of the Smallest Possible Start

Starting is 80% of the battle. The hardest part of working out isn't the workout—it's putting on your running shoes. The hardest part of writing isn't the words—it's opening the document.

David Goggins, a former Navy SEAL and ultramarathon runner, knows this struggle firsthand. In his early twenties, he weighed nearly 300 pounds and was stuck in a cycle of self-doubt. Every time he tried to work out, he felt overwhelmed by how far he had to go. But one day, instead of aiming for a full workout, he gave himself one task—put on his running shoes. That was it.

Once his shoes were on, he thought, *I might as well step outside.* Then, *I might as well jog for a minute.* Before he knew it, he was running.

This method works because it bypasses resistance. The brain doesn't fight small steps. They feel too easy to resist. But once in motion, stopping feels unnatural.

To apply this:

- If you're avoiding writing, tell yourself to write one sentence.
- If you're stuck on cleaning, commit to picking up *one* item.
- If you're procrastinating on studying, just open the book and read a single paragraph.

Now, you might find these actions "so small" and "repetitive". The important thing is that they work. Now, you must do the work too. Small steps remove hesitation. And once you start, you almost always keep going.

Motion Over Perfection

Starting Ugly is Better Than Not Starting at All. Perfectionism is one of procrastination's greatest weapons. It convinces you that if something isn't perfect, it isn't worth starting. The result? Nothing gets done.

Bestselling author Neil Gaiman has written dozens of novels, but he admits that his first drafts are always terrible. He follows a simple rule: *write badly, but write anyway.* The reason? Because a bad draft can be fixed—a blank page cannot.

Ed Sheeran once explained his songwriting process with a plumbing analogy. When you first turn on a faucet after a long time, dirty water comes out. But if you let it run, eventually, the clean water flows. His approach to songwriting is the same—he allows himself to create "bad" songs, knowing that good ones will eventually come.

Annie Duke, a former professional poker player and decision strategist, calls this *resulting*—people wrongly judge decisions by their outcome rather than their process. The key isn't perfection; it's continuous action and refinement.

The lesson is clear: start messy. Get something down. **Progress beats perfection.**

- Instead of waiting for the perfect workout plan, just start moving.
- Instead of crafting the perfect first paragraph, write a terrible one—then improve it.
- Instead of over-researching, begin, and adjust as you go.

Once you accept imperfection, progress becomes automatic.

The Inertia Buster

In physics, an object at rest stays at rest—but an object in motion stays in motion. The same is true for your habits.

World-renowned chef Massimo Bottura, owner of the three-Michelin-star restaurant Osteria Francescana, understands this principle. In the high-pressure world of fine dining, chefs can't afford to hesitate. When the kitchen starts its prep work, Bottura tells his team to follow a simple rule: **never stop moving.**

If you're chopping vegetables, don't pause—move to the next step. If you finish plating a dish, immediately start prepping the next. The kitchen's momentum is never broken.

The same principle applies outside the kitchen. The hardest part of any project is getting started. But once in motion, you stay in motion.

The trick is simple: **always know the next step.**

If you stop and don't know what comes next, inertia builds up again. But if you always leave a clear next action, you stay in motion.

Here's how to apply it:

- When stopping work for the day, leave a note with the next step to start immediately.
- When exercising, always plan the first move before your next workout.
- When cleaning, break tasks into micro-steps, so you never feel overwhelmed.
- Action creates more action. Keep moving, and procrastination doesn't stand a chance.

Fear Slayer

Fear is one of the biggest drivers of procrastination. Not fear in the extreme, life-threatening sense, but in the everyday moments that keep us from taking action—fear of failure, fear of embarrassment, fear of getting it wrong.

Your brain is wired for survival, which means it often views *discomfort* as *danger*. That's why taking the first step on an intimidating project, starting a difficult conversation, or putting yourself out there can feel overwhelming. But here's the truth: fear is a habit, and like any habit, it can be rewired.

The way forward isn't to eliminate fear—it's to change your relationship with it. By shifting your mindset, redefining failure, and conditioning yourself to take small risks, you weaken fear's grip.

. . .

The Experiment Mindset

One of the best ways to neutralize fear is to approach life like a scientist. Scientists don't fear failure—they *expect* it. Every experiment, whether it succeeds or fails, gives them data to improve.

Take Thomas Edison. When working on the lightbulb, he ran thousands of failed experiments. But he didn't view them as wasted effort. Instead, he reframed them, saying: *"I have not failed. I've just found 10,000 ways that won't work."*

Now compare that to how most people approach challenges. Instead of viewing setbacks as useful information, they see them as personal flaws. One rejection means they're *not good enough*. One mistake means they're *bad at it*.

But what if, instead of treating mistakes as proof of failure, you saw them as part of the learning process?

Physicist Richard Feynman adopted this mindset early in life. As a student, he struggled with imposter syndrome at Princeton. But instead of letting fear stop him, he told himself that learning was just experimenting. He approached every challenge with curiosity instead of pressure. This playful mindset helped him win a Nobel Prize.

If you struggle with fear, try this: reframe tasks as experiments.

Instead of:

- *I need to be perfect at this presentation,* say: *Let me test what works and improve for next time.*
- *What if I mess up in this meeting?* say: *Let's see what I can learn from this.*

When you stop treating challenges as high-stakes performances and start treating them as experiments, fear shrinks.

The Worst-Case Game

Your Fears Are (Almost) Never As Bad As You Think. Most fears are illusions. Your mind exaggerates danger, creating worst-case scenarios that rarely happen. Studies show that 85% of the things we worry about never come true. And for the 15% that *do* happen, people handle them far better than they expect.

A public speaker named Scott Berkun learned this firsthand. Early in his career, he gave a keynote speech at a major conference—and it went horribly. He lost his place in his notes, stumbled over his words, and watched as the audience checked their phones.

But here's what he discovered: **it didn't ruin him.** No one mocked him. No one remembered the mistakes. He simply moved on, improved, and kept speaking. Years later, he became a bestselling author and one of the most sought-after speakers in the industry.

Fear makes failure seem catastrophic, but reality is much kinder.

To break fear's illusion, try the **Worst-Case Game**:

1. **Identify what you're afraid of.** Example: Speaking up in a meeting.
2. **Ask: What's the absolute worst that could happen?** Example: You stumble over your words, people think you're nervous.
3. **Now ask: What's the realistic outcome?** Example: A few seconds of awkwardness, then people move on.

Most of the time, the worst-case scenario is minor. And once you realize that, fear loses its power.

Courage Capsules

Courage isn't something you either *have* or *don't have*. It's a muscle. The more you use it, the stronger it gets.

Tim Ferriss, bestselling author of *The 4-Hour Workweek*, has a practice he calls *"fear inoculation."* He deliberately puts himself in uncomfortable situations—like lying down in the middle of a busy sidewalk or wearing ridiculous outfits in public—just to get used to discomfort. Over time, he found that the more he leaned into small fears, the less control fear had over him.

Muhammad Ali used a similar approach. Before big fights, he practiced handling insults and criticism by deliberately sparring with opponents who taunted him. By the time he stepped into the ring, no insult or distraction could shake him.

If you want to become fearless, start with **small courage capsules**—daily actions that condition you to be bold:

- Ask a stranger for directions, even if it feels awkward.
- Share an idea in a meeting, even if your voice shakes.
- Say no to something you don't want to do.
- Post something online without overthinking it.

These tiny acts train your brain to see discomfort as normal. Over time, bigger fears—starting a business, speaking in public, making tough decisions—become easier.

Fear thrives in hesitation. Action kills it. The more you step into discomfort, the more fearless you become.

Quick Micro Wins

You don't need to wait weeks to overcome procrastination. Small, immediate actions can create an instant shift. Here are three simple ways to take control and build momentum right now:

1. **Start with the Five-Minute Rule.** If a task feels overwhelming, commit to doing it for just five minutes. No pressure to finish—just start. Most of the time, you'll keep going because the hardest part is getting started.
2. **Set a Reverse Deadline.** Instead of allowing a task to stretch indefinitely, give yourself an artificial deadline that forces focus. If something usually takes two hours, challenge yourself to finish it in 60 minutes. Shorter time frames prevent overthinking and increase efficiency.
3. **Shrink the Resistance.** When a task feels too big, break it down to the smallest possible action. Write one sentence instead of a full report, put on workout shoes instead of committing to an hour at the gym. Small starts remove mental barriers.

Procrastination isn't a personality trait—it's a habit. And like any habit, it can be broken. Action is the antidote.

Chapter 5

Forging the Iron Will

Mental toughness isn't something you're born with—it's built. The ability to focus under pressure, stay calm in chaos, and push forward when everything feels impossible isn't reserved for a select few. It's a trained skill, one that monks, elite athletes, and military professionals have all mastered.

The secret? *They don't rely on motivation. They condition their minds to act, regardless of how they feel.*

Discipline isn't about forcing yourself through sheer willpower—it's about rewiring your brain to respond differently to stress, discomfort, and setbacks. In this chapter, you'll learn how to sharpen your focus, stay steady in the face of stress, and turn adversity into your greatest asset.

Mental Armor

In a world designed to pull your attention in a thousand directions, focus isn't just a skill—it's a superpower. Those who can control their attention control their results. But focus isn't something you either have or don't have. Like any other skill, it can be trained.

One of the most extreme examples of unwavering focus happened in **1963**, when **Thích Quảng Đức**, a Vietnamese Buddhist monk, set himself on fire in the middle of a crowded street in Saigon. He did not flinch. He did not cry out. He remained in full meditation as flames consumed him. His purpose? A peaceful protest against religious persecution.

Journalists who witnessed the event were stunned—not just by the act itself, but by his complete stillness under unimaginable pain. The monk's ability to remain composed was not luck. It was the result of years of training his mind to master focus and detach from external discomfort.

Though most of us will never need to demonstrate that level of discipline, the principle remains: focus is built through deliberate practice.

A simple way to start is through **focus bursts**—short, structured blocks of deep concentration that strengthen your ability to resist distractions.

Try this:

1. Pick a task and set a **five-minute focus timer**.
2. Remove all distractions—turn off notifications, put your phone in another room.
3. Work with full attention. If your mind wanders, bring it back.

Each time you do this, extend the duration slightly. Over time, your brain adapts, and your ability to focus strengthens. Distraction is a habit. So is focus. Train it daily.

. . .

Mastering the Art of Calm Under Pressure

In high-stakes situations, the difference between success and failure isn't talent—it's control. The ability to *stay calm* when pressure rises is what separates those who thrive under stress from those who crumble.

Jason Redman, a former Navy SEAL, experienced this firsthand. During a combat mission in Iraq, he and his team were ambushed. Bullets tore through his body, but instead of panicking, he relied on a simple but powerful technique: **controlled breathing.**

As chaos unfolded, he slowed his breath—four seconds in, four seconds hold, four seconds out. This technique, known as **box breathing**, calmed his nervous system, kept his mind clear, and allowed him to focus on survival.

The reason it works? Breath controls the brain. When you breathe deeply and slowly, your body lowers cortisol levels (the stress hormone), and your mind regains clarity.

Try this the next time stress spikes:

- Take **three deep breaths**, making your exhale longer than your inhale.
- Use **box breathing**: Inhale for four seconds → Hold for four → Exhale for four → Hold for four.

This technique is used by everyone from SEALs to Olympic athletes. Why? Because it works. Panic is just an untrained response to stress. Train yourself to respond differently.

Turning Setbacks into Strength

Mental toughness isn't just about pushing forward—it's about *what happens when you fall.* Because no matter how disciplined you are, you *will* face setbacks.

The difference between those who stay stuck and those who rise? **How they view failure.**

Michael Jordan, arguably the greatest basketball player of all time, was cut from his high school varsity team. Instead of quitting, he used the rejection as fuel, practicing relentlessly until he became a six-time NBA world champion and one of the most celebrated athletes of all time.

Resilient people don't just endure failure—they *use* it. Psychologists call this **"adversarial growth"**—the idea that setbacks aren't just obstacles, they're opportunities to develop resilience.

Want to train this skill? Keep a **Bounce Log**—a record of every moment you recovered from adversity. Try this:

1. Write down a past failure or challenge which you overcame.
2. Instead of focusing on what went wrong, ask: *What did this teach me?*
3. Identify one way you've grown stronger because of it.

Every time you revisit these moments, you reinforce the truth: you've overcome before—you will overcome again. Mental toughness isn't about avoiding failure. It's about using it as fuel.

Temptation Traps

Discipline isn't just about doing the right thing—it's about making it easier to resist the wrong thing. Every day, you face countless decisions that test your self-control. Should you start working or scroll through your phone? Should you grab fast food or cook something healthy? Stay in bed or get moving?

Most failures of self-discipline don't happen in the moment of action. They happen *before* the decision is even made. If you wait until temptation is in front of you, you've already lost half the battle. The key to beating temptation isn't willpower—it's controlling the conditions that lead to the decision.

Controlling the Outcome Before the Fight Starts

Temptation is hardest to resist when it's right in front of you. That's why most people who struggle with self-control believe they just need to "try harder." But the truth is, the real battle isn't won in the moment of temptation—it's won hours before, when the choice is still in your control.

In the 1980s, Oprah Winfrey was at the height of her career, but she had one struggle she couldn't overcome—late-night snacking. No matter how much she told herself she wouldn't reach for junk food, the craving always won. She tried willpower, but it never lasted.

Then she changed her approach. Instead of *reacting* to temptation, she removed the option altogether. She stopped keeping unhealthy snacks in her house. If she wanted ice cream, she had to drive to a store and buy it. Most of the time, the inconvenience was enough to make her rethink the decision.

By controlling the environment *before* temptation struck, she made discipline effortless.

This strategy works for anything. If you want to stop checking your phone in the morning, charge it in another room. If you want to work out in the morning, lay out your exercise clothes the night before. If you want to eat healthier, plan your meals before hunger kicks in.

Discipline isn't about fighting temptation—it's about removing it.

. . .

Cutting Off Temptation at the Source

Every habit, good or bad, begins with a trigger. If you've ever found yourself eating when you're bored, grabbing your phone without thinking, or lighting a cigarette after a meal, you've experienced this firsthand. Something cues the action—whether it's an emotional state, a time of day, or a specific environment.

This was the biggest challenge for Allen Carr, a British businessman and bestselling author who struggled with smoking for decades. He tried quitting dozens of times but always failed. Then he realized that his addiction wasn't just about nicotine—it was about **association**. His brain had linked smoking to certain activities. Coffee meant cigarettes. Stress meant cigarettes. Finishing a meal meant cigarettes.

Instead of just quitting cold turkey, he tackled the problem at the source. He started changing those associations. Instead of reaching for a cigarette after coffee, he chewed gum. Instead of smoking when he felt stressed, he took a walk. He rewired his triggers, and soon, the cravings faded.

Most people try to fight their triggers with willpower, but a smarter approach is to swap, avoid, or reframe the cue.

If you crave junk food while watching TV, try replacing chips with a bowl of fruit. If social media pulls you away from work, log out of your accounts or use an app blocker. If stress makes you crave alcohol, redefine it as a cue for deep breathing or stretching.

The brain follows patterns. Change the pattern, and the habit follows.

Hacking Your Brain's Dopamine System

Temptation isn't about logic. It's about reward. Every bad habit continues because it *feels good*. Your brain is wired to seek pleasure, and the easiest way to get it is through quick dopamine hits: junk food, social media, binge-watching TV. The problem isn't that you enjoy these things—it's that they hijack your motivation, making real progress feel dull in comparison.

A better example of hacking your brain's reward system comes from Angela Duckworth, the psychologist behind the concept of *grit*. While studying high achievers, she discovered that those who mastered self-discipline didn't rely on deprivation—they learned how to *attach pleasure to productive actions*.

Take marathon runners, for example. Many don't love the pain of running at first. But they learn to associate small wins—completing a mile, beating their personal record, seeing their endurance improve—with satisfaction. Their brains start linking the hard work with pleasure, making the habit easier to maintain.

The same principle works in daily life. Instead of trying to quit social media completely, make real life more rewarding by tracking your personal progress. Instead of eating out for pleasure, turn cooking into a creative challenge. Instead of scrolling your phone for a dopamine hit, pair your hard work with an immediate reward, like listening to music or watching an episode of your favorite show after completing a task.

Dopamine fuels motivation. If you can control where it comes from, you can control your habits. Find creative ways to make the right actions dopamine-filled. For example, one of the best changes I made was to train in the gym at night after a full day of work. Instead of training first thing in the morning, I started to treat it as a reward after a full day of focused work. Incredibly, results not just in my own business improved but performance in the gym too.

The Discipline Muscle

Discipline isn't something you're born with—it's something you build. Like a muscle, it strengthens through resistance, grows when challenged, and weakens when neglected. The problem is that most people avoid discomfort, thinking it's a sign they're on the wrong path. But discomfort isn't the enemy—it's the training ground.

Some of the most mentally tough people in history—monks, athletes, entrepreneurs, and military professionals—aren't special. They've simply trained themselves to handle difficulty in a way that most people haven't. The key is to introduce challenges into daily life, so when real adversity hits, you're already prepared.

Conditioning Yourself for Discomfort

Discomfort is the birthplace of resilience. If you never train yourself to tolerate it, even minor difficulties will feel overwhelming. But if you intentionally expose yourself to controlled discomfort, you become unshakable.

Jocko Willink, a former Navy SEAL commander, built his entire philosophy around the idea that discipline equals freedom. But before he became a best-selling author and leadership expert, he was just a young recruit struggling to push past his own limits. During SEAL training, when exhaustion set in and quitting seemed like the only option, Jocko forced himself to embrace discomfort. He woke up earlier than required, put in extra reps when no one was watching, and leaned into hardship instead of running from it. Over time, his tolerance for struggle increased. What once felt unbearable became routine. His mindset shifted from avoiding pain to using it as fuel—and that shift defined the rest of his life.

You don't have to become a SEAL or put yourself through extreme physical challenges to build a remarkable level of resilience. Small, daily moments of discomfort can rewire your response to stress. A cold shower, delaying your morning coffee by 30 minutes, or pushing yourself to work five minutes past your usual stopping point may seem insignificant, but every time you do it, you train yourself to handle more.

Strengthening Yourself Through Setbacks

The fear of failure holds more people back than actual failure ever will. Most people avoid failure because they associate it with weakness. But failure isn't a sign to stop—it's the process of adaptation in action. Failure is an essential step of success. Try > fail > succeed. You cannot succeed without failing. Taking massive action and embracing failure is the mindset of a winner.

Sara Blakely, the billionaire founder of Spanx, credits her success to a simple mindset shift. Growing up, her father would ask her at the dinner table, *"What did you fail at today?"* If she didn't have an answer, he would express disappointment—not because she had failed, but because she hadn't tried something difficult enough to risk failing.

This reframing changed everything for her. She stopped seeing failure as something to avoid and started seeing it as proof that she was growing. This mindset led her to take risks, test ideas, and ultimately build a billion-dollar brand.

If you want to strengthen your resilience, don't just accept failure—*seek it out in controlled ways.* Instead of avoiding situations where you might fail, lean into them. Speak up in a meeting even if you're unsure. Try a new skill knowing you'll be bad at it in the beginning. Ask for something you're afraid to ask for, even if the answer might be no. Each time you do, you train yourself to detach failure from self-worth, making it easier to take bold action when it matters most.

· · ·

Expanding Your Capacity for Challenge

Growth doesn't come from massive leaps—it comes from gradual expansion. If you push yourself slightly past your limit every day, what once seemed impossible eventually becomes easy.

Shirley Raines, the founder of Beauty 2 The Streetz, didn't set out to build a movement. She simply started by helping one person. Then another. Then another. Her small acts of kindness for the homeless community grew into an organization that now serves thousands.

The key was consistency. She didn't need to do something huge all at once—she just needed to do a little more each day.

Most people set goals that are too extreme and burn out. Real endurance isn't about sprinting—it's about showing up every day, even when progress feels slow. Instead of setting overwhelming goals, push yourself by just 5% more than yesterday. If you're used to working for 30 minutes, push for 32. If you run two miles, go for 2.1. The increase is so small that your brain doesn't register it as difficult, but over time, these tiny expansions create exponential growth.

Quick Micro Wins

1. **Delay gratification for one small pleasure today.** Skip dessert, wait five extra minutes before checking your phone, or hold off on buying something you want. Training your brain to wait makes long-term discipline easier.
2. **Introduce one intentional discomfort into your day.** Take a cold shower, delay caffeine, or finish a task when your mind wants to stop. Each time you push through discomfort, you reinforce the habit of persistence.
3. **Push past your usual quitting point by 5%.** Read for one more page, work for two more minutes, or run a little

farther than planned. Small increases compound into mental endurance.

4. **Reframe failure as progress.** Instead of avoiding failure, look for small ways to practice it. Try something new, ask for something even if the answer might be no, or attempt a skill you know you won't master right away.
5. **Modify one trigger for a bad habit.** If you always check your phone when you wake up, charge it in another room. If you snack out of boredom, put healthier options within reach. Discipline isn't just about resisting temptation—it's about shaping your environment to make success easier.

Discipline isn't about being naturally strong. It's about training yourself to handle more, one small challenge at a time. Now, it's your turn to strengthen yourself!

The Smallest Actions Have the Biggest Impact

"We are what we repeatedly do. Excellence, then, is not an act, but a habit." – Aristotle

Great discipline doesn't just shape individuals—they shape communities. Small actions, done consistently, create massive change. And right now, you have the power to help someone else take their first step toward self-discipline.

Would you help someone just like you—someone who wants to break free from procrastination, build better habits, and take control of their life?

Most people choose books based on reviews. Your feedback could be the reason someone picks up *Micro Discipline* and starts transforming their daily habits.

Leaving a review costs nothing and takes less than a minute, but it could make all the difference for...

- ... one more person ready to finally stop overthinking and take action.
- ... one more entrepreneur struggling to stay consistent in their work.
- ... one more student looking to build better study habits.
- ... one more parent trying to lead by example.
- ... one more dream that might otherwise fade away.

To make a difference, simply scan the QR code or enter the link below and leave a review:

[https://www.amazon.com/review/review-your-purchases/?asin=BOOKASIN]

If this book has helped you, your review could help someone else start their journey. Thank you for being part of this movement.

Jordan Cross

Chapter 6

Invisible Habits

The ultimate form of discipline isn't about forcing yourself to act—it's about making action automatic. The most successful people aren't constantly battling their willpower. They've simply built habits so ingrained that they happen without effort.

She forgot she was disciplined—and that's why she won. Serena Williams is widely recognized as one of the greatest athletes of all time, but what many don't realize is how much of her success came from automatic routines. Before every match, she followed the same sequence: tying her shoelaces a specific way, bouncing the ball exactly five times before a serve, placing her gear in the same precise order. These weren't random habits—they were mental cues that locked her into a state of focus.

When discipline becomes second nature, resistance disappears. This is the goal—not to fight yourself every day, but to create disciplines so automatic that success becomes inevitable.

Habit Loops Unleashed

Every habit follows the same pattern: cue, routine, reward. If you want to make discipline automatic, start by getting clear on the cues that trigger action.

Jessica, a mother of three, struggled with chaotic mornings. She wanted to journal every day but always felt too overwhelmed to find the time. Then she realized she didn't need more willpower—she needed a trigger. She decided that every morning, as soon as she poured her coffee, she would open her journal.

At first, it required effort. But within weeks, her brain made the connection: coffee meant journaling. Soon, she didn't even have to think about it. The habit ran itself.

This principle works for anything. If you want to start exercising, pair it with an existing habit. Keep your running shoes next to your bed and lace them up as soon as you wake up. If you want to drink more water, fill a glass before checking your phone in the morning. If you want to read more, leave a book on your pillow so you pick it up before bed.

Cues eliminate decision fatigue. When set up correctly, your habits will follow automatically.

Making Habits So Simple They're Inevitable

Most habits fail not because they're too difficult, but because they're too complicated. If a habit requires too much effort to begin, your brain will find an excuse to avoid it.

Eliud Kipchoge, the first marathon runner to break the two-hour barrier, understood this deeply. His success wasn't just about hard training—it was about eliminating unnecessary decisions. He ate the same meals every day, trained at the same time, and wore the same shoes. By removing extra choices, he freed up his mental energy for performance.

For disciplines to become automatic, they must be frictionless. The easier an action is, the more likely it is to repeat.

If you want to work out more, sleep in your gym clothes. If you want to eat healthier, prepare your meals in advance. If you want to write more, leave your notebook open on your desk.

Every step between you and your habit is another opportunity for your brain to opt out. Remove the friction, and discipline will take care of itself.

Hacking Your Brain to Lock in Discipline

Every habit, good or bad, exists because your brain expects a reward at the end. This is why scrolling social media, eating junk food, and procrastinating are so difficult to quit—they provide an immediate dopamine hit. If you want good habits to stick, you need to make them rewarding in a way that your brain recognizes.

Maya Angelou, the legendary poet, wrote every day, but not at home. She rented a hotel room where she did nothing but write. Her reward was simple—when she finished, she could go home and relax, knowing her work was done.

If you want a habit to last, tie it to something satisfying.

When you complete a workout, take a cold shower or enjoy your favorite smoothie. When you finish deep work, allow yourself ten minutes of guilt-free relaxation. When you stick to your meal plan, unwind with a book or your favorite show. This is deeply personal and you know yourself best. Going to the gym and train was my reward but for many, it's punishment. No matter how counterintuitive it is, you decide what the reward should be for you.

Here's the key: the reward must be immediate. Your brain won't wait hours or days to feel accomplished. It craves a reason to repeat the behavior now. By reinforcing habits with instant rewards, you increase the likelihood that they will stick.

The habits that last are the ones that feel good. Build them wisely, and soon, they will become invisible.

Stealth Stacking

Some of the most successful people in the world don't rely on motivation or willpower to stay consistent. Instead, they embed good habits into their daily routines so seamlessly that they happen without conscious effort.

Rather than forcing discipline, they attach new behaviors to existing ones—turning ordinary routines into powerful habit loops. This method, known as habit stacking, makes it easy to build discipline without feeling like you're adding more to your plate.

By layering habits, linking behaviors, and piggybacking on routines, you can make progress without even realizing it.

Adding Habits to Existing Routines

One of the easiest ways to build a habit is to attach it to something you already do daily. The more automatic the original habit is, the more likely the new habit will stick.

In college, Bill Gates had a habit of reading before bed every night. This was a non-negotiable part of his routine, so later in life, he used it as an anchor to stack another habit: reviewing his business strategies. Instead of adding a new task from scratch, he attached it to something that was already second nature.

This technique works with almost any habit. If you want to start meditating, do it while your coffee is brewing. If you want to improve posture, straighten your back every time you check your phone. If you want to practice gratitude, say one thing you're grateful for every time you sit down for a meal.

The key is to let the first habit act as a trigger for the second. Once the two behaviors are linked, discipline becomes effortless.

Piggybacking New Habits Without Extra Willpower

One of the biggest reasons people struggle to stay consistent is because new habits feel like additional effort. But what if they didn't? What if they simply *rode the momentum* of what you were already doing?

Chef Massimo Bottura, the owner of the three-Michelin-star restaurant Osteria Francescana, had a rigorous prep schedule that required hours of meticulous ingredient work every morning. Rather than seeing this time as separate from his personal growth, he used it to practice new culinary techniques in small, deliberate ways. He didn't set aside extra time—he integrated learning directly into his routine.

This principle applies to any habit. If you listen to podcasts, switch to one that teaches you something. If you exercise, combine it with audiobooks or language learning. If you're washing dishes, do a few calf raises while you wait for the sink to fill.

When new habits piggyback on old ones, discipline stops feeling like work. Instead, it can feel fun and rewarding just by itself.

Chain Creation

Once you master stacking individual habits, the next step is linking them together into sequences that flow naturally. The best habits aren't isolated—they trigger a chain reaction.

James Clear, author of *Atomic Habits*, describes how he built a fitness habit by chaining behaviors together. Instead of just saying, *"I'll work out,"* he created a sequence:

- Put on workout clothes → Fill water bottle → Step outside → Start running.

By structuring habits in a way that one naturally leads to the next, he eliminated decision fatigue. Once the first step was taken, the rest happened automatically.

This strategy is especially useful for morning and evening routines. It could be as simple as:

- Wake up → Brush teeth → Stretch for two minutes → Do ten push-ups.

Over time, this small chain can grow into a full workout routine. The momentum of one habit will pull the next into place, making consistency effortless.

To build your own chain, start with a cue you already do daily, then attach a small habit, followed by another. The key is to let each action serve as a natural trigger for the next. Once established, this chain of habits will carry you forward without resistance.

The Fade Factor

The highest level of self-discipline isn't about struggle or willpower. It's about automation. The more ingrained a habit becomes, the less effort it requires, until one day you don't even realize you're doing it.

Think about how you brush your teeth. You don't debate whether you *feel like it* each morning—you just do it. It's an automatic behavior, woven so deeply into your life that skipping it feels unnatural.

This is the goal for all high-impact habits. The key to lasting discipline isn't fighting to stay consistent—it's reaching the point where consistency happens *without* a fight.

Autopilot Activation

Studies suggest that over **40%** of daily actions are unconscious habits. That means almost half of what you do isn't a conscious decision—it's a reflex built from repetition.

Take Itzhak Perlman, one of the world's most renowned violinists. By the time he reached adulthood, his daily practice routine was so ingrained that he no longer *thought* about practicing—it was simply part of who he was. His hands knew where to move, his mind slipped into focus, and before he knew it, hours had passed.

This is what happens when habits become automatic.

To test whether a habit has fully faded into autopilot, try the **"fade test"**—skip the habit for a day and see if it feels wrong. If skipping the gym makes you restless, if not journaling feels like something's missing, if failing to meditate makes your mind feel scattered, you've successfully embedded the habit.

At this stage, discipline is no longer something you *do*—it's something you *are*. With that being said, quickly get back to it the next day. Rewiring bad habits could happen just as quickly when you let your guard down.

When Hard Things Stop Feeling Hard

The first time you try anything difficult, it requires an enormous amount of conscious effort. Over time, the amount of effort needed becomes smaller. What once felt unnatural becomes second nature.

This is why frugality becomes second nature to people who have spent years budgeting. At first, they consciously track every dollar. But eventually, saving money stops *feeling* like work—it's just how they operate.

The same thing happens with fitness, productivity, and focus. What was once a struggle *fades* into the background of your identity.

One of the best ways to measure this is by keeping a **fade tracker**—a record of how long it takes for an action to stop feeling like an effort. If it used to take willpower to write 500 words and now it feels effortless, if waking up early is no longer a battle, if eating healthy has become instinctive, you know the discipline has fully taken root.

Discipline isn't just about *forcing* yourself to act. The highest level is about reaching a point where *not* acting feels strange.

Identity Infusion

When a habit is deeply ingrained, it no longer feels like a behavior—it feels like *who you are*.

A common phrase among elite athletes, artists, and professionals is, *"I don't have to force myself to do this. It's just part of me."*

Take Maya Lin, the architect behind the Vietnam Veterans Memorial. She didn't just work in design—she *became* the design. Her mind constantly thought in form and structure, and everything she created reflected her natural way of seeing the world.

This is the final stage of discipline. You don't just go to the gym—you *are* an athlete. You don't just write—you *are* a writer. You don't just practice self-discipline—you *are* disciplined.

At this level, habits are so deeply embedded that removing them would feel unnatural. This is the turning point where success stops being a struggle and starts being a reflection of your identity.

Quick Micro Wins

1. **Test your autopilot habits.** Try skipping a habit for one day and see if it feels off. If it does, you've successfully embedded it into your routine. If it doesn't, reinforce it with stronger cues.
2. **Make one habit easier.** Reduce resistance by cutting steps between you and your habit. If you struggle to write, leave your document open. If you want to read more, keep a book on your pillow.
3. **Track your effort fade.** Keep a log of how difficult a habit feels each week. Over time, notice how actions that once felt hard become effortless.
4. **Reframe your identity.** Instead of saying, "I have to work out," say, "I am someone who takes care of my body." The way you define yourself shapes your habits.
5. **Use habit chaining.** Link new behaviors to automatic ones. If you always make coffee in the morning, chain a short meditation session right after.

When habits become invisible, discipline is no longer a struggle—it's a natural part of who you are. Now, it's time to take things one step further and turn chaos into an ally.

Chapter 7

Chaos as Catalyst

The people who thrive aren't the ones who avoid chaos—they're the ones who *use* it. Some of the greatest breakthroughs in history didn't happen in controlled environments. They happened in the middle of a crisis, in moments of pressure, in situations where failure seemed inevitable.

Disaster birthed his best work. In 1665, Isaac Newton was forced to leave Cambridge University when the Great Plague swept through England. While others panicked, he used the time in isolation to develop some of his most groundbreaking ideas, including the laws of motion and universal gravitation. What could have been a period of stagnation became one of the most productive times in his life. Newton didn't resist the chaos—he turned it into momentum.

If you wait for perfect conditions to take action, you'll never move forward. Instead, you can learn to use disorder as fuel for creativity, adaptability, and resilience.

Embracing the Mess

Albert Einstein developed his theory of relativity while working as a patent clerk, far removed from the structured academic world. J.K. Rowling wrote *Harry Potter* as a single mother, squeezing writing into chaotic moments between raising her child and struggling to make ends meet. The world's best ideas weren't born in perfectly controlled environments—they were forged in unpredictable, messy realities.

If you've been waiting for the "right time" to start a project, build a habit, or change your life, stop waiting. **There is no perfect moment.** Start now, start messy, and adjust as you go. The ability to act *despite* chaos is what sets apart those who succeed from those who never begin.

Why Disorder Sparks Innovation

We're taught to believe that success comes from control, organization, and structured plans. But some of the greatest innovations in history were born out of *constraint and disruption.*

Steve Jobs, co-founder of Apple, was once forced out of the company he built. It was an unexpected, chaotic turn in his career—but instead of seeing it as a dead end, he used it to reinvent himself. During his time away, he started Pixar, which became a revolutionary animation studio, and developed the foundation for what would later become the modern Mac.

Creativity thrives in uncertainty. When the old rules fall apart, new ideas emerge. Instead of resisting chaos, embrace it as a creative catalyst.

Try this: If you're stuck on a problem, **change your environment**. Work in a new location, introduce artificial constraints (set a ridiculous deadline or limit yourself to five words per idea), or flip the problem upside down and ask, *What's the opposite of what I'd normally do?* Sometimes, the messier the situation, the more room for breakthroughs.

Adaptability Trumps Rigidity

The ability to stay disciplined isn't about sticking to a plan at all costs—it's about adapting when the plan falls apart.

During the early days of Airbnb, the company struggled to gain traction. Founders Brian Chesky and Joe Gebbia had a simple plan: rent out air mattresses in their apartment to visitors. But when that didn't scale, they had to pivot—again and again. At one point, they even designed and sold election-themed cereal (Obama O's and Cap'n McCain's) just to keep the company afloat.

Most businesses would have collapsed under the stress, but their adaptability saved them. Today, Airbnb is worth billions—not because everything went according to plan, but because they *adjusted* when things went wrong.

Instead of seeing disruptions as obstacles, treat them as tests of resilience. If something breaks, find a new approach. If an opportunity disappears, pivot toward another. The most disciplined people are not the ones who never change course—they're the ones who know *when* to shift without losing momentum.

Try this: Instead of reacting negatively to unexpected changes, ask, *How can I make this work for me?* Flexibility isn't weakness. It's a skill that makes discipline sustainable.

Sharpening Your Focus Under Stress

Some of the greatest performances, breakthroughs, and creative works happen not in calm environments, but in high-pressure moments.

In the world of fine dining, Chef Gordon Ramsay is known for his ability to remain laser-focused under the chaos of a dinner rush. A busy kitchen, orders piling up, staff moving at high speed—while others crack under pressure, he thrives in it. Instead of being overwhelmed, he uses stress as a focusing tool, heightening his awareness and sharpening his reactions.

Stress can either make you freeze—or force you to focus. The key is learning how to channel it.

Try this: The next time you feel overwhelmed, **slow down instead of speeding up**. Take a deep breath, identify the single most important thing you need to do, and focus only on that. Instead of letting pressure scatter your attention, use it to sharpen your priorities.

Chaos doesn't have to derail you—it can be your greatest asset. When you learn to work with disorder instead of against it, discipline stops being fragile and starts being unbreakable.

Pressure Play

Most people crumble under pressure. Deadlines feel overwhelming, unexpected stress disrupts focus, and urgent situations make it harder to think clearly. But what if pressure wasn't a roadblock? What if it is the very thing that will sharpen your focus, push you into action, and help you perform at your peak?

The difference between those who succeed and those who don't isn't the presence of pressure—it's how they *use* it. Urgency, when harnessed correctly, can be a powerful force that drives discipline and execution.

Urgency Unleashed

Adrenaline sharpens focus. It's why students pull all-nighters before exams, why creatives produce their best work under last-minute pressure, and why athletes perform at their peak in high-stakes moments. Your brain is wired to respond to urgency.

Douglas Adams, author of *The Hitchhiker's Guide to the Galaxy*, famously said, *"I love deadlines. I like the whooshing sound they make as they fly by."* While he joked about it, the truth is that deadlines forced him into action. He once wrote a novel in just three weeks, locked in a hotel room with his publisher ensuring he finished.

Pressure creates focus. Instead of seeing it as an enemy, use it as a *push*. Set artificial deadlines even when none exist. Increase the stakes even if it isn't needed. Make a bet. Put your money on the line. Make it so painful to not achieve your goals.

Channeling Chaos Instead of Fighting It

There's a fine line between pressure that fuels action and pressure that causes burnout. The key is controlled exposure. Just like a muscle grows from *progressive overload*—where stress is gradually increased—mental resilience grows when pressure is managed, not avoided.

The military uses this principle in special forces training. Soldiers are deliberately placed in high-stress environments—sleep deprivation, extreme cold, sudden noise—to simulate real-world conditions. Over time, they learn to remain calm in chaos. The pressure no longer overwhelms them; it becomes normal.

You don't need military training to develop this skill. Start by introducing small doses of controlled pressure into your routine. If you struggle with focus, try working with a Pomodoro timer—set 25-minute sprints of deep work, forcing yourself to make rapid progress. If you want to become comfortable speaking under stress, practice delivering short talks to friends with zero preparation. The more you expose yourself to controlled discomfort, the less chaos will shake you when it arrives unexpectedly.

Turning Time Crunches Into Wins

Not all pressure is bad. In fact, some of the most productive people use it to their advantage by turning deadlines into strategic tools.

Take journalist Hunter S. Thompson. Known for his immersive, high-energy writing, he often worked best under tight deadlines. Instead of writing in long, drawn-out sessions, he used extreme time constraints to force himself into peak focus. His work wasn't the result of endless preparation—it was the product of intense, focused bursts.

You can do the same. If a project feels overwhelming, break it into short, high-intensity sprints. A technique called the **work sprint method** helps you leverage time crunches without burning out. Here's how it works:

1. Set a 90-minute burst to tackle a specific task with full focus.

2. Follow it with a 15-minute break to reset.

3. Repeat up to three cycles per day for deep, efficient work.

This method ensures that you maintain high energy and mental sharpness while still using pressure to drive performance. Instead of seeing deadlines as stressors, turn them into structured challenges that maximize efficiency.

Chaos and urgency don't have to derail you. When used correctly, they can become some of your greatest tools for focus, momentum, and peak performance. The key is to stop resisting pressure—and start using it.

Recovery Rules

Discipline isn't just about pushing forward—it's about knowing how to *recover* when things fall apart. No one operates at peak performance all the time. Even the most disciplined people experience setbacks, burnout, and disruptions. The difference between those who thrive and those who don't isn't whether they face obstacles—it's how quickly they recover.

Elite athletes, top executives, and high performers don't just train hard—they **recover hard**. They have systems in place that allow them to bounce back from stress, regain energy, and turn failures into stepping stones for success. Instead of seeing setbacks as failures, they treat them as *part of the process.*

The goal isn't perfection—it's *resilience*. The faster you recover, the faster you regain momentum.

How to Rebound Fast From Disruptions

Resilience isn't an inborn trait—it's a trainable skill. The ability to bounce back isn't about avoiding failure; it's about knowing how to *recover faster* each time.

In the 2006 Winter Olympics, speed skater Apolo Ohno faced a major setback. In the final stretch of the 1,000-meter race, he was in perfect position to win gold—until a crash wiped out most of the skaters, including him. Instead of giving up, Ohno scrambled to his feet in seconds, crossing the finish line to take silver. His reaction speed and ability to recover from chaos defined his career, earning him eight Olympic medals in his career.

Fast recovery is a skill that can be practiced. The longer you stay down after a setback, the harder it becomes to restart. Instead of letting a disruption throw off your momentum, reset immediately with a small win.

- If you miss a workout, do five push-ups.
- If your schedule falls apart, complete one small task.
- If you break a habit streak, start again *that same day*.

The key to staying disciplined isn't avoiding obstacles—it's refusing to let them stop you.

Why Rest is Part of Discipline

Most people view rest as something you do *after* you've worked hard, but the most disciplined people understand that rest is fuel for peak performance. Burnout doesn't happen because people work too hard —it happens because they don't recover properly.

Arianna Huffington, co-founder of *The Huffington Post*, once collapsed from exhaustion at her desk. She had pushed herself past the breaking point, running on minimal sleep and maximum stress. That moment forced her to reevaluate her approach. She went on to become an advocate for rest as a competitive advantage, proving that sustainable success depends on structured recovery.

The best performers don't just work with intensity—they **recover with intention**. High-level recovery includes:

- **Consistent sleep discipline** (wake-up times, no screens before bed)

- **Physical resets** (movement, stretching, or breathing exercises to clear stress)
- **Mental resets** (journaling, mindfulness, or focused breaks to prevent overload)

Instead of treating rest as a reward, schedule it like a high performer. The more structured your recovery, the more sustainable your discipline becomes.

Turning Setbacks into Stepping Stones

Failure isn't something to *move past*—it's something to *learn from*. Some of the most successful people in history failed more than anyone else, but what set them apart was their ability to turn those failures into **fuel for future wins**.

After launching SpaceX, Elon Musk faced two catastrophic rocket failures, each costing millions of dollars. Most people would have seen these as career-ending losses. Instead, he treated them as data points—learning from every mistake, adjusting, and improving. His next launch? A breakthrough.

Every setback contains a lesson, a pattern, or a miscalculation to correct. The problem is, most people either dwell on failures or ignore them completely. The key to continuous improvement is extracting specific, actionable lessons from every challenge.

Use this **chaos debrief** to analyze setbacks:

1. **What happened?** Identify the root cause.
2. **What could I have done differently?** Pinpoint the mistake.
3. **What's my next move?** Turn failure into a *specific* adjustment.

Instead of fearing failure, use it as feedback. Every mistake contains a key to future success—if you're willing to look for it.

Quick Micro Wins

1. **Reset with a micro-win.** The moment you fall off track, do *something small* to rebuild momentum. If you miss a full workout, do a 30-second plank. If your writing streak breaks, write one sentence. Small wins prevent downward spirals.
2. **Create a personal reset ritual.** Have a go-to recovery habit—a walk, deep breathing, or five minutes of journaling—to shift from frustration back into focus.
3. **Turn failure into data.** Instead of seeing mistakes as personal flaws, treat them like an experiment. Ask, *What did this teach me?* Adjust, then move forward.
4. **Prioritize deep recovery.** Sleep, mental resets, and physical breaks aren't luxuries—they're essential for long-term discipline. Schedule them *before* you need them.
5. **Reduce the gap between failure and action.** The shorter the delay between a mistake and your next move, the faster your progress. Always restart the same day whenever possible.

Discipline isn't just about pushing forward—it's about knowing how to *reset, recharge, and rebuild*. The ability to recover quickly separates those who burn out from those who stay consistent. It's the difference between winning and giving up.

Now the question is: how can you **scale your discipline** to take on bigger challenges without breaking down?

Chapter 8
The Scaling Secret

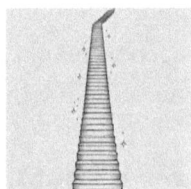

Scaling discipline isn't about doing everything at once—it's about growing strategically. The people who achieve extraordinary results don't start with grand gestures; they start small and expand gradually. One discipline, when compounded over time, can build an empire.

Amazon began as a small online bookstore. Warren Buffett made his first investment at age 11 with just three shares of stock. Serena Williams' career started with basic drills on a public tennis court. None of them achieved success overnight. Instead, they grew their skills, habits, and routines incrementally.

The key to sustainable growth is progressive expansion. Instead of overwhelming yourself with massive leaps, grow in stages. Stack small wins into something far greater.

Amplify Small

Big goals don't require big actions. They require consistent actions that gradually increase in intensity.

Consider fitness. A beginner who attempts an advanced training routine from day one is likely to quit. But someone who starts with one push-up per day and increases the effort slowly can build real strength over time.

One of the best way to scale habits is by using gradual increments:

- Start with a **micro version** of your goal—one push-up, one page of writing, one-minute meditation.
- Increase effort by **5-10% per week** instead of making drastic jumps.
- Track small milestones rather than expecting immediate transformation.

An investor who started investing with just a few dollars per week eventually built a six-figure portfolio using this principle. Instead of going all in, he scaled his investments slowly, allowing discipline and knowledge to develop alongside his finances.

By stretching micro-habits over time, small actions turn into significant transformations.

Stack Scaling

The secret to effortless discipline isn't just growing habits—it's stacking them. Once a habit becomes automatic, it serves as an anchor for the next.

Athletes use this principle when structuring training. Instead of adding random workouts, they combine complementary exercises—strength training with mobility drills, endurance training with speed work. Each layer supports the next.

Scaling discipline works the same way. Once one habit is solid, it becomes a foundation for another.

A mother who struggled to find time for reading started listening to audiobooks while folding laundry. That small change allowed her to consume more books without disrupting her day. Over time, she added new habits—journaling reflections after each book, summarizing key takeaways, then sharing insights with her kids. The habit expanded naturally instead of feeling forced.

To scale habits seamlessly:

1. Identify an existing habit that's already in place—drinking coffee, brushing teeth, checking emails.
2. Attach a small habit to it—stretching after waking up, writing one sentence before checking emails.
3. Expand the habit gradually, layering another once it becomes second nature.

This approach prevents burnout while allowing discipline to develop more effortlessly.

Small Adjustments, Big Results

Scaling isn't always about doing more—it's about tweaking what you already do to make it exponentially more effective.

A struggling writer, for example, might try writing twice as many words per day and fail due to burnout. But if they improve efficiency by just ten percent daily—writing with fewer distractions, refining their process—they could double their output in a few months without added stress.

The same principle applies everywhere:

- A musician who increases practice intensity rather than practice time.

- An investor who optimizes strategy instead of adding more capital.
- A business owner who refines workflows instead of working longer hours.

To apply this strategy:

1. Pick one key area to improve—efficiency, speed, accuracy, endurance.
2. Make a **micro-adjustment**—optimize technique, remove friction, improve focus.
3. Track performance and refine the process.

Instead of overwhelming yourself, refine the small details. Over time, these minor improvements compound into major breakthroughs. Spend time exploring tools like mental models, artificial intelligence and simply searching for solutions online. More often than not, you're simply one search away from your solutions.

The Multiplier Effect

True discipline doesn't just stay in one part of your life—it spills over, amplifying results in unexpected ways. When you improve in one area, the benefits compound into others.

A disciplined fitness routine strengthens more than just muscles—it sharpens focus, increases energy, and boosts confidence. Financial discipline leads to better decision-making in other areas of life. A consistent reading habit improves memory, creativity, and even social intelligence.

Scaling isn't just about doing more—it's about creating *momentum* that makes everything easier.

. . .

Cross-Life Links

Some habits aren't just beneficial in isolation—they act as *keystone habits*, improving multiple aspects of life at once.

Arnold Schwarzenegger didn't just build his career on bodybuilding. His discipline in training translated into his success as an actor, entrepreneur, and politician. The mental toughness required to push through grueling workouts became the foundation for his work ethic in every other field.

A cross-link planner can help identify which habits have the highest return across multiple areas:

- **Exercise boosts productivity.** Studies show that regular workouts improve focus, decision-making, and cognitive performance.
- **Reading sharpens problem-solving.** People who read daily develop stronger analytical thinking, which benefits work, communication, and creativity.
- **Financial discipline strengthens patience.** Learning to delay gratification in spending carries over to career growth, relationships, and long-term goal setting.

By identifying a habit that has broad effects, you can scale your discipline across different areas with much less effort.

How Small Gains Multiply Over Time

Growth isn't linear—it's exponential. A one-percent improvement every day doesn't result in a minor increase. Over time, it compounds into massive gains.

The difference between someone who saves $5 a day and someone who spends that money mindlessly might seem small in the moment, but over a decade, the saver builds financial security while the spender remains stagnant.

This is how small improvements in discipline work. The early results may be invisible, but once they reach a *critical mass*, progress explodes.

Consider the story of Ronald Read, a janitor and gas station attendant who amassed an $8 million fortune—not through luck, but by consistently investing small amounts over time. He didn't try to scale aggressively. Instead, his discipline compounded, growing into something far greater than anyone expected.

The same principle applies to any habit. A writer who improves by ten percent each month will double their output in less than a year. An athlete who increases their endurance slightly each week will outperform their peers over time.

A **multiplier map** can help visualize this:

1. Identify a habit you're already doing.
2. Increase effort by a small, measurable percentage each week.
3. Track progress over a long period, not just short-term gains.

Most people quit too early because they don't see immediate results. The key is understanding that real progress *accelerates*—but only if you stick with it long enough.

How Others Magnify Your Discipline

Scaling doesn't just happen through personal effort—it happens through **social momentum**. The right people can amplify your discipline, while the wrong influences can sabotage it.

This is why top performers surround themselves with others who push them higher. Successful entrepreneurs network with other driven individuals. Elite athletes train in competitive environments. Writers and creatives seek out accountability partners.

One study on habit formation found that **when people pursue goals alongside a supportive community, they're far more likely to stay consistent**.

The right environment accelerates growth:

- Friends who prioritize health make fitness easier to maintain.
- A workplace that values focus makes deep work feel natural.
- A group that reads together encourages lifelong learning.

In the 1950s, six friends in Omaha, Nebraska, formed an investment group called the "Buffett Partnership." One of those friends? Warren Buffett. Being surrounded by financially disciplined individuals helped sharpen his investment philosophy, setting him on the path to becoming the world's greatest investor.

To leverage a network boost:

1. **Find like-minded individuals** pursuing similar habits.
2. **Create accountability**—weekly check-ins, shared challenges, or friendly competitions.
3. **Help others scale, too**—by teaching and encouraging, you reinforce your own discipline.

Together, progress accelerates.

Sustainability Shift

Growth is exciting. Progress is addictive. But unchecked scaling can lead to collapse if you don't know when to pause, recharge, and sustain momentum.

Many high achievers push too hard, assuming that more effort equals more results. But in reality, overloading leads to burnout, decline, and even quitting altogether. The key to long-term success is not just acceleration—but knowing when to maintain and recover.

Scaling isn't just about doing more—it's about pacing yourself to sustain performance for the long haul.

Knowing When to Pause Growth

Scaling too fast without structure often leads to **diminishing returns**. A business that expands beyond its capacity too quickly will collapse under the weight of its own growth. The same applies to personal discipline—if you stretch beyond your limits, your habits suffer, and consistency crumbles.

Elon Musk is famous for his extreme work ethic, but even he has admitted that long-term overwork comes with a cost. During the early days of Tesla, he was sleeping in the office, working nearly 120 hours a week. Eventually, his health and decision-making suffered. He later reduced his workload, emphasizing that sustained productivity requires smarter effort, not just harder work.

To prevent burnout, use a **load check** system:

- If motivation is dropping sharply, pause and assess workload.
- If performance is declining despite effort, adjust the pace instead of pushing harder.

- If exhaustion sets in, schedule a period of maintenance instead of growth.

Scaling doesn't mean full-speed expansion at all times. Smart discipline means knowing when to hold steady before the next leap forward.

Why Recovery is the Key to Longevity

In athletics, the highest performers don't just train hard—they rest strategically. Coaches build in active recovery periods to prevent injuries and sustain peak performance.

Science backs this approach. Studies show that short breaks increase productivity by up to 30%, while prolonged overwork leads to diminishing returns. Even in creative fields, rest is essential. Salvador Dalí, one of the most famous surrealist painters, took intentional micro-naps to keep his mind fresh and ideas flowing.

A well-balanced **rest rhythm** includes:

- Micro-breaks throughout the day to reset focus.
- Deliberate pauses after periods of intense work.
- Full recovery days to prevent burnout.

Instead of fearing rest, see it as a performance multiplier. The best performers don't just work hard—they recover just as hard.

Turning Stability into Strength

Most people see plateaus as failure, but in reality, plateaus are where strength is built.

A long-distance runner doesn't increase mileage indefinitely. They hold steady at a certain level before making another push. This period of maintenance allows the body to adjust, adapt, and prepare for the next challenge.

Bruce Lee, one of the most disciplined martial artists of all time, didn't train at maximum intensity every day. He built rest and reflection into his process, understanding that pushing too hard would lead to injury and stagnation. He knew that progress happens in waves, and plateaus are an essential part of mastery.

To sustain success:

- **Recognize that pausing isn't failure**—it's a strategy.
- **Use plateaus to refine skills** instead of abandoning effort.
- **Prepare for the next growth phase** by maintaining consistency.

Scaling isn't just about speed—it's about sustainability. The best performers are those who know when to push and when to pause.

Quick Micro Wins

1. **Set a maintenance phase.** Instead of always pushing forward, schedule periods where you focus only on maintaining progress. This prevents burnout and strengthens discipline.
2. **Track effort, not just results.** If performance is dropping despite effort, reassess your workload before forcing more output.
3. **Use the 80% rule.** If you feel exhausted, work at 80% capacity instead of stopping completely. Small efforts prevent regression.

4. **Schedule proactive recovery.** Instead of waiting until burnout, plan rest periods in advance—just like top athletes do.
5. **Redefine plateaus as preparation.** If you feel stuck, shift focus to refining skills rather than abandoning habits.

Scaling like a pro means knowing when to accelerate and when to sustain. Growth isn't about going all-out at all times—it's about lasting long enough to reach the highest levels.

Chapter 9
The Forever Framework

Some people burn bright for a few years and then fade. Others stay consistent for decades, becoming stronger, sharper, and more disciplined as they age. The difference? They don't chase quick wins—they build a foundation that lasts a lifetime.

Discipline isn't just about what you do today—it's about making sure your habits can evolve, sustain, and strengthen over time. Longevity isn't about maintaining *one* routine forever. It's about designing systems that adapt to life's changes while keeping core principles intact.

At 80 years old, Warren Buffett still wakes up at the same time every morning, reads for hours, and follows the same daily investing habits he developed in his youth. His methods have evolved, but the foundation remains unshaken. That's the power of a forever framework.

Lifelong Loops

Discipline isn't about sticking to rigid rules forever—it's about making adjustments that allow habits to grow with you.

Take fitness. A person who thrives on intense workouts in their 30s might need to shift to low-impact strength training in their 60s to maintain movement without injury. The key isn't doing the *same* thing forever—it's keeping the habit alive in a way that matches your phase of life.

An 82-year-old named Ed Whitlock shattered records in long-distance running, becoming the oldest person to run a marathon in under four hours. But he didn't train the same way at 80 as he did at 40. Instead of pushing high-intensity workouts, he adapted by running at a slow, sustainable pace for hours every day, proving that consistency beats intensity over time.

To ensure your discipline last, build flexibility into your routines:

- If a habit feels unsustainable, scale it to match your energy levels.
- If physical limitations arise, find alternative ways to practice discipline.
- If life circumstances change, adjust routines instead of abandoning them.

Discipline should be future-proof—designed to last even when circumstances shift.

The Unshakable Pillars of Discipline

While many habits will evolve over time, a few should remain **non-negotiable**—the *core anchors* that keep you grounded no matter what changes around you.

At 98 years old, world-renowned neurologist Dr. Brenda Milner still goes to work every day. Her research on memory shaped modern neuroscience, and her commitment to intellectual growth never wavered. Her career evolved, but her core anchor—lifelong learning—stayed intact.

The key to long-term success isn't maintaining *everything*—it's knowing which habits are *too valuable to lose*. These are the anchors that, no matter what happens, should never be abandoned.

A **forever list** helps identify these:

- What routines make you feel the most focused, healthy, or sharp?
- Which habits have given you the most long-term benefits?
- What practices keep you grounded no matter how life changes?

Your core anchors will sustain you through every phase of life. Warren Buffett is still famously "tap-dancing" to work. Find what you love and don't stop. First you fuel your discipline. Then, your discipline fuels you.

The Key to Longevity in Discipline

One of the biggest reasons people lose discipline isn't because they lack willpower—it's because they fail to adapt when life shifts.

A new parent who used to meditate for 30 minutes daily might not have that luxury anymore. But instead of quitting, they could adjust to five-minute meditations while the baby naps.

A corporate executive who retires might struggle with structure. Instead of losing their routine, they can pivot discipline toward personal projects or new learning opportunities.

The people who maintain discipline longest find creative ways to pivot instead of quitting.

When Japanese educator and philosopher Shigeaki Hinohara turned 75, he redesigned his life structure to prioritize health, movement, and daily intellectual stimulation. He lived to 105, working and writing until the end. His secret? He adjusted his habits with every decade, keeping discipline alive in different forms.

A **pivot playbook** helps prepare for life's transitions:

1. **Identify major changes ahead** (career shifts, aging, family changes).
2. **Redefine routines**—if something no longer fits, adjust rather than abandon.
3. **Stay committed to core values**—the *form* of discipline may change, but the *principles* remain.

The most successful people aren't rigid—they evolve, ensuring their habits last as long as they do.

Discipline isn't just for now—it's for life.

By designing habits that evolve with age, anchoring core principles, and learning to pivot when needed, you can build a **forever framework** that keeps discipline alive no matter where life takes you.

The Relapse Remedy

Even the most disciplined people stumble. Athletes miss workouts, entrepreneurs lose motivation, and even the most focused individuals admit to moments of distraction. The difference between those who succeed long-term and those who quit isn't that the successful never fail—it's that they know how to recover quickly and keep moving forward.

A lapse doesn't mean everything is lost. The ability to course-correct swiftly is what separates lifelong discipline from short-lived motivation. If you've ever abandoned a habit after missing a few days or let a minor failure spiral into a major setback, you're not alone. The problem isn't the slip itself—it's letting it grow into something bigger. The key to lifelong discipline is catching small mistakes before they turn into complete relapses, bouncing back with simple actions, and moving forward without guilt.

Catching the Slip Before It Becomes a Fall

A single skipped workout doesn't erase months of progress, but repeated skips can reset a person back to zero. A missed writing session won't ruin a book, but consistent avoidance leads to abandoned drafts. When one mistake turns into two, then three, a new habit forms—a habit of stopping.

People don't fail because they mess up once. They fail because they let the slip go unnoticed until it's too late to regain momentum.

In weight loss studies, researchers have found that those who regain weight after dieting often follow a predictable pattern: one "cheat meal" turns into an entire week of poor eating, and instead of correcting the behavior early, they justify continued indulgence. The real problem isn't the first mistake; it's the failure to correct course when things start slipping.

One of the best ways to avoid this downward spiral is through **early awareness**. Recognizing when discipline is breaking down is the first step in preventing a full relapse. Signs to look for include declining enthusiasm for a habit, justifications that start creeping in— "I'll get back on track tomorrow" or "One time won't matter"—and disruptions in routine.

The sooner these warning signs are acknowledged, the easier it is to reset before losing too much ground.

Bouncing Back With Small Steps

Once a habit is broken, many people believe they need to compensate for lost time. A runner who misses three days of training might try to push themselves through an extreme workout to "make up" for the lapse. A student who falls behind on studying may attempt an all-night cram session to get back on track. This mindset often leads to burnout and failure because it places unnecessary pressure on the comeback.

Meb Keflezighi, a professional marathon runner, suffered an injury that kept him from training for months. Instead of trying to return at full intensity, he started with small, manageable sessions, gradually rebuilding his endurance. A year later, he won the Boston Marathon, proving that slow, steady returns lead to lasting success.

The fastest way to recover from a lapse isn't to push harder—it's to restart in the smallest, simplest way possible. Writing just one sentence after missing several days of work is better than attempting to finish an entire chapter in one sitting. A single push-up after skipping workouts for a week is better than an unsustainable two-hour gym session.

The key is **momentum over intensity**. When getting back on track, focus on:

- Restarting with the smallest version of the habit to remove resistance.
- Avoiding self-punishment—the goal is to regain rhythm, not to suffer through excessive effort.
- Committing to the next action instead of dwelling on the mistake.

No comeback has to be perfect. Embrace the beauty in the imperfection. Focus on getting back to being consistent.

Letting Go of Guilt and Moving Forward

Many people don't just struggle with falling off track—they struggle with how they see themselves after a setback. They shift from "I skipped my workout" to "I'm lazy." They go from "I procrastinated on this task" to "I can't stay focused." This type of negative self-talk reinforces failure, making it harder to recover.

Self-compassion, rather than self-criticism, has been shown to be one of the strongest predictors of long-term success. Studies suggest that those who forgive themselves for mistakes are more likely to resume their habits, while those who dwell in guilt tend to fall further into inactivity.

J.K. Rowling, before becoming one of the most successful authors of all time, faced multiple failures and rejections. Instead of seeing setbacks as proof that she wasn't capable, she treated them as part of the process, focusing on learning rather than self-blame.

One of the most effective ways to move past a relapse is to **reframe failure as feedback**. Instead of thinking, "I failed, so I'm not disciplined," ask, "What can I learn from this?" Identifying what caused the slip—whether it was exhaustion, stress, or a lack of planning—turns the mistake into a lesson.

Guilt doesn't rebuild habits. Action does. The sooner the focus shifts from regret to the next step, the sooner discipline can be restored.

Discipline Isn't About Never Slipping—**It's About Never Stopping**

Lapses are inevitable. What matters isn't avoiding failure—it's mastering recovery. By catching setbacks early, returning to habits in the simplest way possible, and moving forward without guilt, discipline becomes something that lasts.

Legacy of Control

At some point, discipline becomes more than just a personal practice—it becomes something that shapes the world around you. The most disciplined people don't just transform their own lives; they **leave a lasting impact on others**.

A life of discipline isn't just about what you achieve. It's about the habits, lessons, and mindset you pass on. Whether through mentorship, influence, or the example you set, your commitment to discipline extends beyond you.

Every great leader, teacher, and innovator carries this responsibility. Their discipline didn't just fuel their success—it *rippled outward*, changing the lives of those who followed.

Passing Discipline to Others

Teaching something is one of the fastest ways to solidify your own mastery. When you mentor someone—whether it's a friend, a colleague, or your own child—you reinforce the very habits you want to keep.

A father who teaches his children the value of self-discipline doesn't just shape their future; he strengthens his own discipline. A leader who instills focus in a team doesn't just improve productivity; they hold themselves to a higher standard.

Many of history's greatest minds understood this. Benjamin Franklin, one of the most disciplined figures in history, didn't just keep his structured habits to himself—he mentored others, wrote about self-improvement, and ensured his lessons endured beyond his own lifetime. His 13 *Virtues*—a self-imposed code of discipline—became a model for generations to follow.

To teach discipline effectively:

- Lead by example—people don't follow words, they follow actions.
- Share lessons in a way that makes them accessible.
- Offer mentorship and accountability to those who need guidance.

When you teach discipline, you ensure that its impact outlasts your own lifetime. Share the ideas in this book that you've tried and have helped you the most. Your personal story can be the greatest inspiration for the people around you. Share the "Quick Micro Wins" which you found most helpful. Something magical happens when you teach. You automatically level up that which you teach.

Measuring the Reach of Your Influence

It's easy to overlook how small habits create big ripples. A single act of discipline—waking up early, committing to deep work, staying consistent—can inspire others in ways you may never see.

A schoolteacher introduced his students to simple yet powerful goal-setting habits, never realizing the lasting impact it would have. Decades later, many of those students looked back and credited those lessons with shaping their careers and personal lives. What started as a small classroom practice became a ripple effect, influencing generations of success.

Discipline isn't just about self-improvement—it's about the unseen impact. A mentor's words might inspire a breakthrough. A book on productivity might change a reader's habits for life. The way you live could inspire the way others think and act.

Take inventory of your own impact:

- Who has been influenced by your discipline or even lack of it?
- How have your habits affected others—directly or indirectly?
- What lessons have you passed down without realizing it?

Every disciplined action leaves a footprint—sometimes in ways you'll never fully know. One noble goal is to strive to be an example, not a warning. We do not want to waste years of our lives, to ultimately become a walking warning to the next generation.

Building a Legacy That Outlives You

What does discipline look like decades from now? How will your habits continue to shape the world long after you're gone?

Those who leave the greatest impact think beyond themselves. Their discipline isn't just about personal achievement—it's about ensuring that their work, values, and mindset continue long after they're gone.

The legendary investor Charlie Munger spent decades refining his principles of decision-making, focus, and rational thinking. But he didn't just use these for his own success—he shared them through speeches, writings, and mentorship. Long after his passing, his insights continue to shape investors, entrepreneurs, and thinkers.

To create a lasting legacy of discipline:

- Think in decades, not just days—what habits will serve you long-term?
- Document what you've learned—journals, books, or even small notes can outlast a lifetime.

- Plan what comes next—what will you build, teach, or share to keep discipline alive beyond your own journey?

Eternity starts today. The actions you take now set the foundation for something greater than yourself.

Quick Micro Wins

1. **Write down your core principles**—Even if no one reads them today, they may guide someone in the future.
2. **Be the example**—Your habits, routines, and discipline will inspire others more than any words ever could.
3. **Teach a small habit to someone younger**—A simple lesson can become a lifelong practice for them.
4. **Reflect on your impact**—Take inventory of how your discipline has influenced others and what you want to continue sharing.

Discipline isn't just for you—it's for everyone who follows in your footsteps. Your commitment to discipline, consistency, and focus can create ripples that outlast a single lifetime.

Chapter 10

Mastery Unleashed

Hopefully, the person who began this journey is not the same person reading this now.

When you started, discipline may have felt like a struggle—something you had to force yourself into, something that required effort, something outside of your natural instincts. Hopefully with each chapter, from building habits, to overcoming setbacks, to scaling your discipline, you're no longer just "trying" to be disciplined anymore. I hope: **You are disciplined now.**

Mastery is never about external validation or perfection—it's about *owning* discipline as part of who you are. The final stage of this journey is not just about maintaining habits. It's about operating at a level where discipline is second nature.

You've done the work. Now, let's step into the mindset of someone who commands their disciplined self with ease.

The Mastery Mindset

At the highest levels of any field—sports, business, the arts—there is a common trait among masters. They don't think of discipline as something they "do." They think of it as **who they are**.

Elite athletes don't need to convince themselves to train. Successful writers don't debate whether to sit down and create. They do these things because they have **internalized** their discipline. It's no longer a choice—it's part of their identity.

Muhammad Ali once said, *"I am the greatest. I said that even before I knew I was."* His words weren't arrogance; they were a reflection of his belief in himself long before the world recognized his mastery. His confidence wasn't external—it was something he built from within.

Your identity drives your actions. If you see yourself as someone who struggles with focus, you'll always fight against distraction. But if you see yourself as a disciplined, structured, and focused individual, every action you take will align with that identity.

Take ownership of your mindset:

- **Affirm your discipline daily.** A simple belief—*"I am disciplined"*—can reshape how you act. You know my favourite. "I do it NOW" works magic for me.

- **Eliminate self-doubt.** Discipline is not about being perfect; it's about consistency.
- **Stop "trying"—start being**. When you no longer have to force discipline, you've mastered it.

Remember, you think, therefore you win. Even if it seems unbelievable right now, believe that you are *that* person, that disciplined self.

Confidence Compound

Every success—no matter how small—reinforces confidence. The more times you follow through on discipline, the stronger your belief in yourself becomes.

Psychologists call this *self-efficacy*—the belief in your own ability to succeed. It's one of the strongest predictors of long-term achievement. Those who trust their ability to stay disciplined will outperform those who constantly doubt themselves.

Consider the transformation of Mel Robbins. She struggled with anxiety and procrastination, constantly feeling stuck. One day, she introduced a simple rule: **counting down from five before taking action.** The *5-Second Rule* became a habit, then a lifestyle, then a global movement that helped millions overcome procrastination.

What started as a tiny win, which for Mel was getting out of bed on time, became the foundation for complete confidence and transformation. Building confidence through discipline follows this formula:

1. **Small actions lead to small wins.**
2. **Small wins lead to consistent success.**
3. **Consistent success leads to unshakable belief.**

To solidify your confidence, build a *proof pile*—a collection of past achievements that remind you of your discipline. Every time you hesitate, revisit your successes, no matter how small.

Mastery isn't about talent or luck—it's about proving to yourself, over and over and over and over and over and over again, that you are capable.

The Ceilings You See Are Illusions

The final stage of discipline is realizing that there are no limits to what you can achieve.

Most people operate within artificial constraints—self-imposed beliefs about what they are *capable* of, what they *deserve*, and what is *realistic*. These limits are not real. They are constructs of habit, environment, and past conditioning.

Arnold Schwarzenegger grew up in a small Austrian village. No one from his hometown had ever done anything remarkable, and yet, as a child, he decided he would become the greatest bodybuilder in the world. He did. Then he decided he would be a Hollywood star. He did. Then he became the governor of California.

His success wasn't about natural talent or connections. It was about refusing to accept limitations. Ask yourself:

- What would I pursue if I knew I couldn't fail?
- If I could be the most disciplined version of myself, what would I achieve?
- Where in my life am I *limiting* myself based on false assumptions?

The same discipline that got you here, to this page, is the discipline that will break past your current ceiling. The future is wide open, and discipline is the key to unlocking its full potential.

It's Who You Are

Mastery isn't about perfect execution. It's about reaching a level where discipline is no longer a struggle. You don't need to force it. You don't need motivation. You don't need reminders. You are disciplined because you see yourself as disciplined. You do the hard things, even when you don't feel like it. You focus on micro wins, and they turn into macro victories. It's simply who you are.

This is the highest level of success—not just understanding discipline, but **becoming it**.

Procrastination's Grave

The version of you who hesitated, overthought, and delayed action no longer exists.

Procrastination is not a personality trait—it's a learned behavior. And like any habit, it can be replaced. In its place, you've built a system that makes action your default response. The shift is profound: no more waiting for motivation, no more wasted time in indecision. Just movement, momentum, and completion.

The disciplined don't wait. They start. They finish. They leave no task undone. This is where you bury procrastination forever.

Action as the Default Setting

Hesitation is just procrastination disguised as caution. The longer you pause before a task, the harder it becomes to start. The mind builds resistance, spinning excuses until action feels impossible.

Consider the story of Richard Branson, the billionaire entrepreneur behind Virgin Group. He didn't build an empire by overanalyzing every decision—he took action, often before he felt "ready." When he started Virgin Atlantic, he had no experience in the airline industry. The idea came to him when his flight was canceled, and instead of complaining, he chartered a plane, filled it with passengers, and turned the experience into a business.

His philosophy? **"Screw it, let's do it."** He understood that waiting for the perfect moment only leads to missed opportunities.

Procrastination dies when you take away its oxygen: **indecision.** The moment you recognize hesitation, act immediately. Small actions lead to small wins. Small wins compound into unstoppable discipline.

The rule is simple: **If you feel the urge to delay, act within five seconds.**

No thinking. No analyzing. Just move.

The Power of Quick Starts

Research from behavioral psychology reveals a powerful truth: *the longer you delay a task, the more difficult it becomes to start.* Every moment spent overthinking creates additional resistance.

Professor Piers Steel, author of *The Procrastination Equation*, found that people who initiate tasks quickly—even if imperfectly—are far more likely to finish them than those who try to "prepare" before starting.

A well-known example of this principle comes from James Dyson, the inventor of the Dyson vacuum. He didn't spend years theorizing about how to build the perfect prototype. Instead, he built over **5,000 failed prototypes** before creating his first successful design. He moved fast, learned from action, and refined his process through doing, not waiting.

Another case: a software engineer named Ryan struggled for years to finish personal projects. He would get excited about an idea, then procrastinate on execution. One day, he set a **first-five sprint rule** before doing anything else in his day, he would spend the first five minutes making immediate progress on a project. No pressure, no expectations—just a commitment to begin.

Those five minutes always turned into something more. A quick start bypasses the mental friction of beginning. If a task feels overwhelming, shrink it down to just the first five minutes. That's all it takes to break through inertia.

Burying Incomplete Work Forever

Unfinished work clutters the mind. It lingers in the background, creating stress and draining mental energy. Loose ends demand attention, leaving you stuck in a cycle of open loops.

This principle is rooted in the **Zeigarnik Effect**, a psychological phenomenon where unfinished tasks consume more mental bandwidth than completed ones. This explains why people feel anxious about lingering to-dos, even if they aren't actively working on them.

Take the example of Sheryl Sandberg, former COO of Meta. Known for her relentless execution, Sandberg applied a rule she called **"done is better than perfect."** She understood that perfectionism leads to procrastination, so she focused on completing tasks rather than endlessly refining them. This approach helped her scale teams, launch projects efficiently, and maintain high productivity without burnout.

Another example: Jessica, a working mother, constantly felt overwhelmed by household tasks, work deadlines, and personal goals. Her breakthrough came when she implemented a **"done daily" tracker**—instead of adding more tasks to her list, she committed to **completing** something each day. Whether it was finishing a work project, closing an open email thread, or completing an errand, she made sure tasks were put to rest.

If something isn't worth finishing, it's worth letting go. If it matters, bury hesitation and get it done.

Success Redefined

Discipline was once the bridge between where you were and where you wanted to be. Now, it's simply part of you. But what's next? What happens when you no longer have to fight for discipline—when it becomes effortless, automatic?

The answer is **freedom**.

Success is not just about achieving external milestones. It's about internal mastery—knowing that no matter what challenges arise, you have the power to navigate them. This chapter is about redefining success on your terms, unlocking true freedom, and ensuring your impact outlives you.

You've built the foundation. Now, let's elevate it into something even greater.

You Own the Definition of Success

For most people, success is a moving target. They achieve a goal, only to replace it with a new one. They reach a milestone but feel unfulfilled. That's because they never stopped to define **what success actually means to them.**

Without a clear vision, you risk chasing a life that was never meant for you.

Take the story of Howard Schultz, the man behind Starbucks. Growing up in a poor neighborhood, his early definition of success was simple: escape poverty. But as he built a billion-dollar company, he realized financial success wasn't enough. He wanted to create a company that treated employees like family, that offered healthcare and opportunities to those from humble beginnings. His vision of success evolved, and instead of chasing endless growth, he focused on making a meaningful impact.

Success is deeply personal. Ask yourself:

- What do I actually want—not what society tells me to want?
- If I removed status, money, and external validation, what would success look like?
- What kind of work, relationships, and life would make me proud?

You have the discipline to achieve whatever you set your sights on. Now, set your sights on something that actually matters to you.

Discipline Unlocks True Liberty

At the start of this journey, discipline may have felt like restriction—a set of rules limiting what you could do. But in reality, discipline is what makes **freedom possible**.

The most disciplined people in the world are also the freest. Why? Because they have control. Control over their time, their habits, their actions. They aren't slaves to distractions, impulses, or emotions.

Tim Ferriss, author of *The 4-Hour Workweek*, realized this firsthand. He initially chased success in the form of financial wealth, working long hours and burning himself out. But over time, he saw that true success wasn't about working more—it was about **owning his time**. He automated his business, eliminated unnecessary tasks, and built a life where he could spend months traveling while still thriving professionally.

Freedom isn't about escaping work. It's about designing a life where work, rest, and passion coexist on your terms.

Take a moment to list what freedom means to you. Maybe it's having the time to travel. Maybe it's financial independence. Maybe it's being fully present with family, or the ability to pursue creative passions without financial stress.

Whatever your answer, discipline is the key to unlocking it. When you control yourself, you control your future.

What Will You Leave Behind?

The final stage of discipline isn't just about personal success. It's about impact.

True mastery isn't measured by how much you accomplish—it's measured by how much you influence others.

Take Nelson Mandela. He endured 27 years in prison, but he never let his mind or spirit be broken. He emerged stronger, using his discipline and resilience to lead South Africa out of apartheid. His success wasn't just his own; it rippled across generations.

You don't need to change the world on a global scale. Your legacy might be the lessons you pass down to your children, the business you build that supports your community, or the example you set for those who look up to you.

Consider:

- What message do I want my life to leave behind?
- What lessons can I pass down that will outlive me?
- How can I use my discipline to create a lasting impact?

Success isn't about how much you gain. It's about how much you give back.

Quick Micro Wins

To fully integrate this chapter's lessons, try these small but powerful actions:

1. **Write Your Success Statement.** Define success in one clear sentence. Example: *Success to me means having full control over my time, doing work I love, and making a positive impact on others.*
2. **Create a Freedom List.** Write down three things you want more freedom in (e.g., time, finances, creative work). Then, list one disciplined action that will help you achieve each.
3. **Set a Legacy Goal.** What do you want to leave behind? Identify one habit, project, or mindset shift that will create a lasting impact.
4. **Do a Success Audit.** Review your current goals. Are they aligned with your true definition of success, or are they based on external expectations? Adjust them accordingly.

Conclusion: The Micro Legacy

One small discipline can rewrite your life.

Maybe it started with waking up ten minutes earlier. Maybe it was saying no to distractions. Maybe it was forcing yourself to start, even when you didn't feel like it. Whatever the habit was, it can spark something bigger than you expect.

Now, hopefully you don't just think about self-discipline—you live it.

Maybe you've transformed from someone who struggled with inconsistency, procrastination, and self-doubt into someone who shows up, follows through, and thrives. Maybe you've built an inner foundation so strong that no setback, no temptation, no external force can shake it. Or maybe you're still on your journey towards self-mastery. Either way, kudos to you!

So, what's next?

This isn't the end of your journey. It's the beginning of a new way of life.

The Transformation You Created

Think back to when you first picked up this book. You might have felt like discipline was something you lacked. Maybe you struggled with procrastination, self-doubt, or inconsistency. You wanted control over your habits, your time, and your future, but somehow, it always slipped away.

Now, things are different.

Every chapter of this book was a stepping stone—from breaking down mental sabotage to redefining self-discipline as a system, not a struggle. From overcoming procrastination to scaling habits that made discipline effortless. The person reading this final chapter is not the same person who started Chapter One.

You've learned how to turn chaos to control, hesitation to action, scattered effort to focused mastery.

The shifts made weren't massive overnight changes. They were **micro**—small, strategic, and relentless.

If you could go back and talk to your past self, what would you say? Would you reassure them that discipline was never about being perfect, just about showing up consistently? Would you tell them that motivation was never the answer, but systems were? Would you prove to them that the smallest habits would change everything?

The End of Delay

Procrastination doesn't define you anymore.

Once, you hesitated before big projects. You put off hard things because they felt overwhelming. You waited for motivation, energy, or the "right time." But now? You act. You start before you feel ready. You take small steps and let them build.

Reflect on your first real **win**—the first time you applied one of these principles and saw it work. Maybe it was using the "five-second rule" to stop hesitating. Maybe it was the "first-five sprint" to build momentum. Maybe it was finishing a long-avoided task just because you told yourself, *"Done is better than perfect."*

That win wasn't a one-time thing. It was the **beginning of a new pattern**.

Now, your default response to hesitation is action. Procrastination has no power over you anymore. It's buried. Forever.

The Compounding Power of Habits

The small actions you once underestimated have now stacked into something undeniable.

Think of the habits you've built—the micro-missions that seemed insignificant at first but compounded into something massive. Maybe you started writing just 50 words a day, and now you're consistently journaling, blogging, or finishing projects. Maybe you began with five minutes of daily exercise, and now you've built a fitness habit that's second nature.

The math is simple: **1% improvement every day = 37x improvement in a year**.

Success isn't a sudden breakthrough. It's a slow build that becomes unstoppable. Now, you are living proof that small habits matter. Celebrate that.

Because what started as a spark is now a fire. And fires don't go out easily.

Living Micro

You no longer have to force discipline. It flows naturally.

The best part? This isn't just about work, goals, or habits. It applies to everything—your relationships, your health, your mindset, your ability to push through life's challenges.

The One-Minute Challenge

If you want to ensure this lasts forever, here's your final challenge:

Every single day, complete one micro action that reinforces your discipline.

It can be as simple as:

- Making your bed with full attention
- Doing one more rep at the gym
- Writing one extra sentence
- Saying no to one distraction
- Holding yourself to a higher standard in a small way

Small actions, every day. This is how you keep the **micro fire** alive.

Mindset Meld

When people struggle with discipline, they often believe it's about what they *do*. They think it's about forcing habits, pushing through resistance, or following strict routines.

But real discipline isn't about *what you do*. It's about **who you are**.

The disciplined don't rely on external forces. They don't need constant motivation or accountability. They've merged who they are with how they act.

This is now your identity.

The moment you say, "I am disciplined," and act accordingly, everything shifts. It's no longer about willpower—it's about alignment.

A tree doesn't try to grow. It just grows. You don't try to be disciplined. You just are.

System Sustain

How do you ensure this momentum never fades? By maintaining the system.

Every great performer, from athletes to entrepreneurs, understands that mastery isn't about reaching a peak and stopping—it's about staying in motion.

- **Check your habits regularly**—are they serving you or do they need adjustment?
- **Keep scaling**—when habits feel too easy, increase the challenge.
- **Eliminate distractions before they creep in**—discipline isn't just about doing, it's about protecting what matters.

You're not just disciplined for today. **You're disciplined for life.**

Inspire Others

Every person who masters discipline has a responsibility—not just to themselves, but to others. You now have something rare: real control over your actions, habits, and mindset.

That control can change the lives of those around you.

Someone in your life is now struggling with the same things you once did. They battle procrastination, inconsistency, and frustration daily. They might even believe that they are trapped.

Show them that they are not.

You don't have to preach or lecture. Just **be** the example. Let them see your consistency, your self-control, your ability to push forward. Because when they see you transform, they'll believe it's possible for them too.

Worldly Wins

Small habits don't just change individuals. They change the world. Every great movement, invention, and transformation started with one person deciding to be disciplined.

Imagine if more people applied these principles.

- If leaders led with discipline instead of impulse.
- If students truly understood consistency early.
- If businesses focused on long-term excellence over short-term wins.

The world isn't changed by huge leaps. It's changed by small, daily, disciplined actions that compound over time.

That means **your part matters**.

Even if you only change your own life, the impact spreads further than you think.

What you've built here won't just last a month or a year. It will last a lifetime. Discipline is the one trait that outlives all others. It doesn't fade like motivation. It doesn't crumble under pressure. It doesn't get taken away by luck or circumstance. It stays.

And when you pass this down—whether to your children, your team, or the people who look up to you—it will outlive you. This is your legacy.

Your discipline will **echo** beyond you.

The revolution doesn't end here.

It begins now.

Keeping the Momentum Alive

Now that you have the tools to build unshakable self-discipline, crush procrastination, and take control of your habits, it's time to pass that knowledge forward.

By sharing your thoughts on *Micro Discipline*, you'll help other readers—just like you—find the same guidance they need to finally take action and create lasting change.

Most people discover life-changing books through reviews. Your honest feedback could be the reason someone picks up this book and starts transforming their daily routines.

Thank you for being part of this movement. Self-discipline grows stronger when we share what works—and you're helping me do just that.

If this book helped you, I'd be incredibly grateful if you could leave a review. Simply scan the QR code below or visit this link:

[https://www.amazon.com/review/review-your-purchases/?asin=BOOKASIN]

Your words could be the spark that ignites someone else's journey.

Jordan Cross

Bonus: Summary & Micro Wins

Each chapter ended with small, powerful actions—Micro Wins—that reinforced discipline. Hopefully, these actionable takeaways helped you to integrate self-discipline into daily life. Below are even more ideas of Quick Micro Wins from each chapter accompanied by a quick refresher on what the chapter is about.

Chapter 1: The Sabotage Code

Goal: Identify and eliminate the hidden forces that sabotage discipline.

1. Perform a Distraction Audit – Identify your top three distractions (e.g., phone, social media, environment) and eliminate or reduce them.

2. Set Up Micro Defaults – Pre-decide common choices in advance (e.g., pre-plan meals, work outfits, or study times).

3. Create a Digital Fortress – Turn off notifications, enable "Do Not Disturb," or remove time-wasting apps.

4. Declutter Your Workspace – Clear your desk or workspace for mental clarity and focus.

5. Reframe Fear as a Signal to Act – When you feel fear or hesitation, take one small step forward immediately.

Chapter 2: The Micro-Mission Mindset

Goal: Shrink the battlefield—use small wins to build momentum.

1. The 10-Second Rule – Pick a task and do 10 seconds of it immediately.

2. Reduce the Goal by 90% – Instead of "write 500 words," commit to writing 50. Instead of "exercise for 30 minutes," start with 3.

3. Track One Micro-Habit for 7 Days – Pick one habit and commit to tracking it daily for a week.

4. Stack a Tiny Habit Onto an Existing Routine – Attach a new habit to something automatic (e.g., stretch after brushing your teeth).

5. Use the Two-Minute Rule – If something takes less than two minutes, do it immediately.

Chapter 3: The Effortless Engine

Goal: Make discipline automatic—remove friction and build seamless systems.

1. Create a Five-Minute Morning Routine – Design a simple, repeatable routine to start your day with clarity and momentum.

2. Make a Habit Foolproof – If a habit requires too much effort, make it easier (e.g., sleep in gym clothes to remove morning resistance).

3. Batch Decision-Making – Decide once, execute multiple times (e.g., plan meals for the week instead of deciding daily).

4. Reduce Environmental Friction – Place cues in your environment that support good habits (e.g., keep a book on your pillow to read at night).

5. Use a Done List – Instead of focusing on a to-do list, write what you accomplished at the end of the day to reinforce progress.

Chapter 4: Procrastination's Kryptonite

Goal: Defeat procrastination—turn deadlines into allies.

1. Set a Reverse Deadline – Choose an end date, then work backward to break it into smaller deadlines.

2. Use the 5-Second Rule – When you feel the urge to delay, count 5-4-3-2-1 and start immediately.

3. Start with a Five-Minute Sprint – Work on something for just five minutes—momentum will carry you forward.

4. Shrink the Task to the First Action – Instead of "write a report," just write the first sentence.

5. Create a Visible Progress Tracker – Use a calendar, journal, or app to mark daily progress.

Chapter 5: Forging the Iron Will

Goal: Strengthen willpower by mastering discomfort and resilience.

1. Take a 30-Second Cold Shower – Train your mind to stay calm under discomfort.

2. Do One Uncomfortable Thing Daily – Push your limits slightly (e.g., hold eye contact longer, say no to distractions).

3. Create a "Stress Reset" Routine – When overwhelmed, pause and take three deep breaths before reacting.

4. Track a Streak for 30 Days – Pick a habit and don't break the chain (e.g., 30 days of journaling or no sugar).

5. Use the "What If" Method – When facing fear, ask: *"What if this works?"* instead of *"What if I fail?"*

Chapter 6: Invisible Habits

Goal: Make discipline effortless—transform habits into autopilot behaviors.

1. Pair a New Habit with an Old One – Link a new habit to an existing one (e.g., do push-ups after brushing your teeth).

2. Create a Habit Loop – Set a cue (alarm), an action (exercise), and a reward (a small win celebration).

3. Use the "2-Minute Rule" for Automation – If a habit feels too hard, shrink it to something that takes two minutes or less.

4. Make Success Automatic – Remove decisions by making discipline part of your identity (*"I am the kind of person who..."*).

5. Use a Habit Scorecard – Rate your habits weekly—what's working, what's not? Adjust accordingly.

Chapter 7: Chaos as Catalyst

Goal: Turn stress and unpredictability into fuel for progress.

1. Reframe Stress as a Challenge – Instead of "I have to do this," say "I get to do this."

2. Use Constraints for Creativity – Limit time or resources to force focus (e.g., 30-minute writing sprint with no edits).

3. Set a Controlled Crisis – Give yourself an urgent deadline for tasks that need motivation.

4. Practice "Planned Disruptions" – Occasionally work in new environments or conditions to build adaptability.

5. Use a Recovery Ritual – When life gets chaotic, have a structured reset routine (e.g., deep breaths, journaling, or a short walk).

Chapter 8: The Scaling Secret

Goal: Expand discipline without burnout—grow habits exponentially.

1. Increase Effort by 1% Each Day – If you're doing 10 push-ups, add 1 more daily. If reading for 10 minutes, increase by a minute.

2. Stack a New Habit on a Successful One – If you meditate daily, add 5 minutes of stretching after.

3. Use the "Tiny Tweaks" Method – Improve systems with small upgrades (e.g., batch tasks to save time).

4. Track Growth, Not Just Completion – Measure improvement (e.g., run faster, lift heavier, work more efficiently).

5. Mentor Someone in Discipline – Teaching reinforces learning—help someone build a habit you've mastered.

Chapter 9: The Forever Framework

Goal: Maintain discipline for life—avoid burnout and sustain progress.

1. Perform a Habit Check-In Monthly – Evaluate what's working and what needs adjusting.

2. Schedule a Weekly Reset – Reflect, plan, and realign priorities every Sunday.

3. Use "Off Seasons" to Recharge – Take breaks to avoid burnout while maintaining structure.

4. Create a Personal "Success Constitution" – Write down your core habits, values, and guiding principles.

5. Never Break Two Days in a Row – If you miss a habit one day, get back on track immediately.

Chapter 10: Mastery Unleashed

Goal: Fully integrate discipline into your identity—become unstoppable.

1. Live by the Identity Rule – Instead of *"I want to be disciplined,"* say "I am disciplined."

2. Set a Legacy Goal – Choose one habit, project, or mission that will have a lasting impact.

3. Audit Your "Shoulds" vs. "Musts" – Drop obligations that don't align with your true vision.

4. Teach One Habit to Someone Else – Reinforce discipline by sharing what you've learned.

5. Celebrate Your Mastery – Look back at how far you've come, and recognize that you're never going back.

References

Books on Habits, Discipline, and Behavior Change

Baumeister, R. F., & Tierney, J. (2011). *Willpower: Rediscovering the greatest human strength.* Penguin.
Clear, J. (2018). *Atomic habits: An easy & proven way to build good habits & break bad ones.* Avery.
Duhigg, C. (2012). *The power of habit: Why we do what we do in life and business.* Random House.
Goggins, D. (2018). *Can't hurt me: Master your mind and defy the odds.* Lioncrest Publishing.
Newport, C. (2016). *Deep work: Rules for focused success in a distracted world.* Grand Central Publishing.
Thaler, R. H., & Sunstein, C. R. (2008). *Nudge: Improving decisions about health, wealth, and happiness.* Yale University Press.

Scientific Studies on Self-Discipline, Procrastination, and Habit Formation

Baumeister, R. F., Bratslavsky, E., Muraven, M., & Tice, D. M. (1998). *Ego depletion: Is the active self a limited resource?* Journal of Personality and Social Psychology, 74(5), 1252–1265. https://doi.org/10.1037/0022-3514.74.5.1252
Duckworth, A. L., & Seligman, M. E. (2005). *Self-discipline outdoes IQ in predicting academic performance of adolescents.* Psychological Science, 16(12), 939-944. https://doi.org/10.1111/j.1467-9280.2005.01641.x
Gollwitzer, P. M., & Sheeran, P. (2006). *Implementation intentions and goal achievement: A meta-analysis of effects and processes.* Advances in Experimental Social Psychology, 38, 69-119. https://doi.org/10.1016/S0065-2601(06)38002-1
Mischel, W., Ebbesen, E. B., & Zeiss, A. R. (1972). *Cognitive and attentional mechanisms in delay of gratification.* Journal of Personality and Social Psychology, 21(2), 204–218. https://doi.org/10.1037/h0032198
Muraven, M., & Baumeister, R. F. (2000). *Self-regulation and depletion of limited resources: Does self-control resemble a muscle?* Psychological Bulletin, 126(2), 247–259. https://doi.org/10.1037/0033-2909.126.2.247
Steel, P. (2007). *The nature of procrastination: A meta-analytic and theoretical review of quintessential self-regulatory failure.* Psychological Bulletin, 133(1), 65–94. https://doi.org/10.1037/0033-2909.133.1.65
Wood, W., & Rünger, D. (2016). *Psychology of habit.* Annual Review of Psychology, 67, 289-314. https://doi.org/10.1146/annurev-psych-122414-033417

References

Key Statistics and Studies Referenced in the Book

- 92% of New Year's Resolutions Fail:

Norcross, J. C., Mrykalo, M. S., & Blagys, M. D. (2002). *Auld Lang Syne: Success predictors, change processes, and self-reported outcomes of New Year's resolvers and nonresolvers.* Journal of Clinical Psychology, 58(4), 397–405. https://doi.org/10.1002/jclp.1151

- 1% Daily Improvement Leads to 37x Growth in a Year:

Originally referenced in Clear, J. (2018). *Atomic habits: An easy & proven way to build good habits & break bad ones.* Avery.

- Average Person Checks Their Phone 150+ Times a Day:

Andrews, S., Ellis, D. A., Shaw, H., & Piwek, L. (2015). *Beyond self-report: Tools to compare estimated and real-world smartphone use.* PLoS ONE, 10(10), e0139004. https://doi.org/10.1371/journal.pone.0139004

- Multitasking Lowers Productivity by 40%:

Rubinstein, J. S., Meyer, D. E., & Evans, J. E. (2001). *Executive control of cognitive processes in task switching.* Journal of Experimental Psychology: Human Perception and Performance, 27(4), 763–797. https://doi.org/10.1037/0096-1523.27.4.763

- Cluttered Environments Reduce Focus:

McMains, S., & Kastner, S. (2011). *Interactions of top-down and bottom-up mechanisms in human visual cortex.* Journal of Neuroscience, 31(2), 587–597. https://doi.org/10.1523/JNEUROSCI.3766-10.2011

- Dopamine's Role in Habit Formation and Procrastination:

Volkow, N. D., Wang, G. J., Fowler, J. S., Tomasi, D., & Telang, F. (2011). *Addiction: Beyond dopamine reward circuitry.* Proceedings of the National Academy of Sciences, 108(37), 15037–15042. https://doi.org/10.1073/pnas.1010654108

www.ingramcontent.com/pod-product-compliance
Lightning Source LLC
Chambersburg PA
CBHW060611080526
44585CB00013B/784